KOMA KULSHAN:

The Story of Mount Baker

SUNRISE ON MOUNT BAKER

KOMA KULSHAN:

The Story of Mount Baker

John C. Miles

Chuckanut
Editions

Bellingham, Washington

Koma Kulshan: The Story of Mount Baker
©2010 by John C. Miles. All rights reserved.
Revised & Expanded 25th Anniversary Edition
published by Chuckanut Editions, Bellingham, WA.

Text updates and a host of new photos included.
New map by Stefan Freelan.
2nd edition design, layout and cover by Kathleen R. Weisel.

Originally published by The Mountaineers in 1984 / Published
simultaneously in Canada by Douglas & McIntyre.
Original book design by Elizabeth Watson.
Original layout by Marge Mueller.
Original maps by Katy Callaghan Huston.

Printed in the United States of America.

Cover: Lowe party—the first photograph
taken on Mount Baker, by W.O. Amsden.

Library of Congress Cataloging in Publication Data

Miles, John C.
    Koma Kulshan

    Bibliography: p.
    includes index.
    1. Baker, Mount, Region (Wash.)—History. 2. Mountaineering—
Washington (State)—Baker, Mount, Region—History. I. Title.

ISBN 978-0-9842389-3-4

For Rotha
who loved and explored
this place with me.

Mount Baker and Iceberg Lake.

A mountain's life is a man's life multiplied by billions, but not a changeless infinity. The mountains call us, not to rest, but to work. A great peak is a frowning challenge, until we have scaled it; a strong and trusted friend thereafter. We can share in the life of the mountain; we can search its history until we are as old in knowledge as it is in experience; we can stand on its summit and be lifted up in spirit as if we had grown to its height and expanded in soul to the whole reach of a broadened horizon. The glaciers have carved a castle for us whose ceiling the sun emblazons with cubic miles of filmy gold; the winds fling banners from the bleak peaks; the winters of ages have piled our partitions; the summers of centuries have grown the pines for our bedposts, and God has scattered the firmament with stars, to give us courage by contemplating their infinity, to measure our pygmy finitude against the giant but also finite mountains. The torrents and the pines sing to us, the birds and the busy squirrels speak to us, the rocks preach to us, and the mind is at stress with the muscles as the soul breathes deep with the lungs. So the mountains enter into our lives as we enter into theirs. We are lifted up in the high places, not beyond ourselves, but to our best selves.

Chester Rowell, 1921

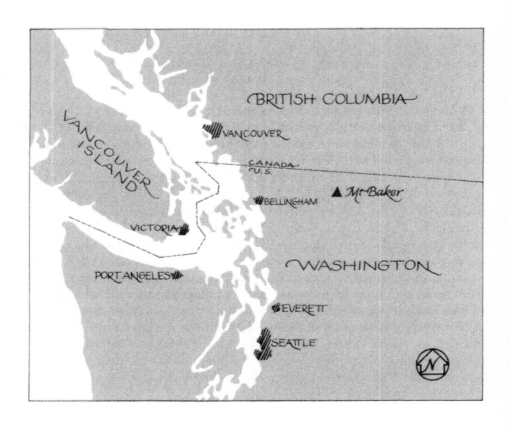

Contents

Snow camping, Mount Baker in the background.

Preface

Mount Baker is not a large mountain compared with the giants of the world, but it is a dominant landform where it stands. In northwestern Washington, people speak generally of the "Mount Baker region" and refer to indeterminate areas according to their proximity to the high white bulk of ice, snow and rock towering five thousand feet above its foothills. On clear days our eyes are drawn to the volcano on the horizon. People in downtown Vancouver and Victoria, British Columbia, in Bellingham, Port Townsend, Everett, and even Seattle, Washington share its majesty. Mount Baker and other volcanoes scattered down the Cascade Range have been focal points for human attention and activity for more than a century.

The era of human interest in the mountain is but the blink of an eye in its history. Mount Baker is approximately four hundred thousand years old (or young, in view of the earth's four-billion-year history). Indians gazed upon Koma Kulshan, as some of them referred to it, for perhaps ten thousand years before Euro-Americans came to the region. It was a place of forbidding mystery to them, though they climbed its flanks in search of mountain goats and berries. European explorers came late in the eighteenth century and noticed the mountain, but many years passed before anyone was motivated to venture upon it.

Mountaineering as a sport began early in the nineteenth century, and eventually climbers came to the glaciers of Mount Baker. The topographer Henry Custer passed close to it, as did prospectors, but they were busy with other pursuits. An Englishman, a man who climbed mountains for sport, finally rose to the challenge and climbed to Mount Baker's summit. Edmund T. Coleman and his companions were the first of thousands who have by now explored every possible route on the mountain's many glaciers and faces.

The story of Mount Baker is not, however, only the story of mountaineering on its heights. It is also a story of exploration and development, of prospecting and mining, of logging and government forest management, of promotion and preservation. It is a story of triumphs and tragedies, of Joe Morovits who explored and prospected and went away broke, of Harvey Haggard who trained and raced and won a marathon, of six college students who died in an avalanche. Above all, the Mount Baker story tells of a slow opening of a wilderness. It is a microcosm of the story of mountains in the American West. The story begins in a vast, virtually untracked wilderness,

Alpenstocks were used for support by those on the 1908 Mountaineers summit climb.

and it ends, at least in its telling here, with wilderness still present but greatly diminished. It begins in a time when the wilderness of North America was so vast that it seemed unlimited, in a time when wild country was an obstacle to be overcome. The story unfolds to the present, when wild country around Mount Baker is valued by many precisely because it is wild, when at least part of the people who know the place see in it values other than the minerals and timber that early pioneers saw there.

The inspiration for this book came from Charles Finley Easton, the Bellingham jeweler who spent thirty years of his life as a part-time student of Mount Baker. Easton loved the mountain and wanted to share it with other people. To this end he wrote and talked endlessly to anyone who would listen. He promoted the idea of a Mount Baker National Park. He compiled a huge scrapbook of Mount Baker information and memorabilia, offered as Exhibit A in his efforts to promote a park. This treasure was available for browsing at the Whatcom Museum of History and Art for decades after his death. I came upon Easton's "book" and it provided the inspiration and foundation to pursue a Mount Baker book of my own, for many of the same reasons that motivated him.

For Easton, climbing was joy. Studying the mountain gave him an excuse to climb it. He thought the mountain inspirational and worthy of attention for its unusual beauty. He was fascinated with the natural history of the place, particularly the glaciers, and wanted to know as much as he could about its many dimensions. I share all of those motivations with him.

Easton also seems to have been interested in promoting development of the Mount Baker region. He was a leader of the Mount Baker Club, the avowed goal of which was to attract public attention to the peak, principally through the Mount Baker Marathons, so that roads would be built and tourist trade would flourish. The idea of a Mount Baker Lodge was at least in part his. His promotion of a Mount Baker National Park was not born of a preservationist leaning but because a park would attract much attention and lead to tourist development and economic growth for the region. Some of Easton's promoter's dreams have been realized, but Mount Baker is not in a national park though some today still think it should be.

Much of the Mount Baker story is, of course, about mountaineers and mountaineering. Mount Baker is not at the center of ordinary human enterprise but is on the periphery. Most people who have encountered the mountain directly have done so for the fun and challenge of it. They have been mountaineers or skiers. Some have been pioneers of their sports – Coleman, Fred Beckey and Ben Thompson. Most have been in search of excitement and adventure who cared not that they followed in someone else's footsteps. For them, meeting the physical and emotional challenge of the climb and

Coleman Pinnacle and Mount Baker.

knowing that they had climbed that big mountain on the horizon has been enough satisfaction.

Most climbers have enjoyed their adventure and returned unscathed. A few have not been so fortunate. Part of this story is tragic and heroic, of people being hurt or killed, and of people rescuing those in trouble. There have been remarkably few accidents in view of the multitudes that have walked upon Mount Baker in a century of activity. But the tragic part of the story must be told, if only to establish that a trip to this mountain is not to be taken too lightly.

Koma Kulshan was originally conceived as an encyclopedic treatment of Mount Baker. It was to deal with natural as well as human history. But natural history, fascinating as it is, would be distracting; it is the backdrop against which the human story is played. Mount Baker's natural history can be pieced together from several excellent sources. The complete story of its natural history deserves its own book.

This project has been possible only with the help of many people, though only I can be held responsible for any errors that might appear. I am especially indebted to librarians at the Bellingham Public Library, the Western Washington University Library and The Mountaineers Library. The staff at the Whatcom Museum of History and Art was most helpful, as were United States Forest Service people at the Glacier Ranger Station and the Supervisor's Office of the Mount Baker-Snoqualmie National Forest. The Mount Baker Hiking Club gave me access to their extensive scrapbooks, and Gary Haufle and Archie Lawson were especially helpful. George Mustoe, Tom Highberger, Fred Beckey, Alan Millar and Diane Cornell read the manuscript of the original edition,and offered helpful suggestions. Al Hugo offered inspiration and assistance with photographs. Brenda Hascall patiently typed the manuscript of the original edition, and Laurie Winfield edited it.

Jeff Jewell, curator of the photographic collection at the Whatcom Museum has been a huge help in the revision which required locating and digitizing as many of the original photographs as possible. Ruth Steele at Western Washington University's Center for Pacific Northwest Studies, and Tamara Belts at the University Library's Special Collections were also helpful with photographs. Candace Wellman offered new information on John Tennant. Chuck Robinson encouraged this revised edition and is publishing it. I thank him for his support and his nagging!

My wife Rotha and daughter Jacki tolerated and encouraged the grumpy author through the years that I originally struggled with this project. My friend and colleague Susan Morgan helped me in myriad ways with the revision. I thank them and all the others who have made this book possible.

*Edmund Coleman's depiction of the final few feet to the summit on his
1868 first ascent.*

1

The First Ascent

Mount Baker is the most northerly of those great cones which dot the Cascade range . . . like another "Snowy Olympus," it towers above, the silent sentinel of a solitary land. . . .

– Edmund T. Coleman, 1869

Edmund Thomas Coleman was a tall and slender man of polished manner and gentle demeanor. A native of England, born in 1824, he was a librarian, a botanist and an accomplished artist. He was also a mountaineer, a charter member of the Alpine Club (London) who had climbed in the Alps and published work in which he described and illustrated the Mount Blanc massif. For unclear reasons, but most likely because he had exhausted his once considerable financial resources, he left England in 1862 and moved to Victoria on Vancouver Island, a community established nineteen years earlier as a Hudson's Bay Company fort. He claimed to have made the move because he was ". . . determined to leave the beaten paths of the European ice-fields for the unexplored heights of the west."[1]

If he had come to Vancouver Island to climb mountains, there could have been little doubt in his mind which mountain he should climb. There on the eastern horizon, gleaming white on cloudless days, like Mont Blanc, was Mount Baker. Other mountains could be seen in all directions, but none stood out so dramatically as this one. He wrote of it:

> Above all, it displays those towering masses, ever marked features of the earth, but pre-eminently conspicuous on this coast. These have their culminating point in Mount Baker, one of the great peaks of the Pacific. . . . It is remarkable for its beauty of outline bears a considerable resemblance in this respect to the Jungfrau, the queen of the Bernese range of the Alps . . . . The height of this mountain is rendered the more apparent from the circumstances

of there being no other peaks in the immediate neighborhood to dwarf it, and also from the comparatively low height of the hills intervening between the spectator and its base.

Perhaps Coleman came to Victoria rather than some other British colonial town because of Mount Baker. He was familiar with the narrative of Captain Vancouver's voyage to the West Coast, with its engraving of Mount Rainier. He might also have read Richard C. Mayne's description of British Columbia, published in England in 1862. In Mayne's book was an engraving of Mount Baker.[2] Whatever motivated him to come to Victoria, Coleman found himself staring across at the mountain as he went about his daily work as a librarian.

By 1866 he was ready to tackle Mount Baker. Time was pressing him. He was forty-two years old. He was also "jaded and depressed, sick of the monotonous round of my ordinary occupations." On July 19, 1866, Coleman crossed from Victoria to Port Townsend in the Washington Territory to join a Dr. Robert Brown of Edinburgh, Scotland, and Charles Benjamin Darwin, a United States magistrate assigned to the territory. The three men, passengers in an Indian canoe, made for the delta of the Skagit River, thinking it would provide them with a route to the base of the mountain.

The river presented a few obstacles. Six miles upstream from its mouth they came upon a huge log jam requiring three exhausting portages. The brush was very thick and mosquitoes were at their midsummer peak. Coleman, Brown and Darwin persisted, making their way up the river to where the Baker River comes in from the north. Knowing that their route must go up this river, they sought guides among the Indians living there. But not only were the natives unwilling to serve as guides, they refused to let the white men go any further. The party was forced to give up their attempt; Coleman and Brown returned to Victoria.

Coleman was undaunted. Two days later he again boarded the steamer to Port Townsend and once more set out for the mountain. This time he went north to Bellingham Bay to ask local people about the best route to the mountain. He discussed prospects with Edward Eldridge, a local pioneer. Eldridge convinced him that the best approach would be up the Nooksack River, which flowed from the very base of the peak. Eldridge assured Coleman that he would not encounter unfriendly Indians as he had on the Skagit; he knew members of the Lummi and Nooksack tribes living along the proposed route and agreed to help procure Indian canoes and other assistance.

Coleman recruited two local men to join him on the climb, both prospectors who had traveled close to the mountain six years before. John Bennett was a Scotsman who had arrived in the infant community of Sehome eight

Coleman party on the Nooksack River in their "shovel-nosed" canoes.

years before on his way to what he hoped would be richly reward labors in the gold fields of Canada's Fraser and Thompson rivers. (Sehome, one of three small communities on Bellingham Bay, would eventually become part of the city of Bellingham.) Riches eluded Bennett as they did so many gold-seekers, so he soon returned down the gold rush trail to Bellingham Bay to settle. Trained as a botanist, Bennett decided that one prudent path to riches would be to nurture his passion for plants into a business. He worked in the coal mines in Sehome, saved his money and bought land which he turned into a plant nursery. This venture was progressing nicely when Coleman came along and, while visiting the Eldridges who lived next to Bennett's property, invited him to join the attempt to climb Mount Baker.

Bennett, Coleman and Eldridge went to the mouth of the Nooksack River, where they procured canoes and Indian guides and started up the river. A few miles upstream they encountered a log jam. Coleman undoubtedly hoped this one was not a bad omen. While the Indians worked the canoes around the jam, Bennett and Coleman walked to the cabin of John Tennant in hopes of persuading him to join the group.

John Bennett

Tennant was quite a character and Bennett knew him as a fellow horticulturalist and as a local politician. He had arrived in the area sometime in the mid-1850s from Arkansas where he had been educated as a civil engineer. Drawn to the west and to adventure like so many young men at this time, he joined a cattle drive that took him all the way to northern California near Lassen Peak. He had made his way to Sehome, working as a surveyor in the mine there and likely reading law under local attorney E.C. Fitzhugh, a common way to attain a legal education in those days. Accepted into the bar in 1860, he served as a legislator and, a bachelor, was given the name "The Black Prince" in a poem written by Olympia schoolgirls. Tennant

John Tennant

was smart and hard-working and during his career not only farmed, botanized, and legislated but was a sheriff, a Mason, and even a minister. When Coleman and Bennett approached him about joining their expedition to Mount Baker in 1866, he was married to Clara, daughter of the chief of the Lummis. Himself part Indian, he was on good terms with the local natives, knew the language, and would be a great asset to the party. Coleman, having been turned back by the Indians south of the mountain, hoped for a different result with the Indians of the Nooksack Valley, and Tennant could help establish good relations with them.

Coleman, Tennant, Bennett and their Nooksack Indian assistants made their way up the river. Travel was difficult: the river was shallow and swift, not good for upstream canoe travel. With great effort they struggled to the present site of Glacier and turned up the milky Noochsakatsu (now called Glacier Creek) toward the mountain. Seven miles of extremely hard going brought them to the foot of what came to be known as Coleman Glacier, which they climbed, according to Coleman, to a saddle at its top. Tennant

Thomas Stratton

was taken ill at snow line, and Coleman and Bennett climbed the glacier. From the saddle the pair ascended northeastward up the cone, only to be stopped by "an overhanging cornice of ice . . . [a] perpendicular wall . . . . A wall of ice." They knew they were near the summit, but the hour was late. They decided to retreat to the saddle with hopes of trying the last bit again the next day.

Their night was miserable "without blankets, and with only a small keg of cold tea to quench our raging thirst." Their "camp" was cold at nine thousand feet – both men "were forced to keep moving all night to keep from freezing." Despite their fatigue they tried again the next morning but again were stopped by the steep ice and conditions "very dangerous on account of avalanches and sliding ice." Coleman's disappointment, being denied success so close to his goal, can be imagined. He was probably near the top of what is now called the Roman Wall, a mere two hundred feet below the summit. Unable to circumvent its difficulties because of fatigue and lack of provisions and time, Bennett and Coleman returned once again to the saddle, where they planted what they had hoped would be the summit flag, along with a "pain killer" bottle, and turned back down the mountain. Rejoining Tennant and their two guides, they enjoyed a wild ride down the Nooksack, marveling at the skill with which the Indians ran the rapids. Safely reaching the mouth of the river, Coleman was unable to find Indians to paddle him to Victoria. He spent two weeks with Eldridge, sketching scenes of the area, and finally returned to Victoria on September 5. He had spent a month and a half trying to climb Mount Baker.

Two years later Coleman was back on the shores of Bellingham Bay. Indians had brought him and David Ogilvy through the San Juan Islands from Victoria by canoe. Ogilvy, reportedly an experienced climber in his early thirties, had been hired by Coleman to assist in what he intended this time to be a complete ascent of Mount Baker. These two were joined at the home of Edward Eldridge by Thomas Stratton, the Customs Inspector in Port Townsend, whom Coleman had invited to join the expedition. The adventurers enjoyed the frontier hospitality of the Eldridge family and their friends. When it was time to depart, a farewell ceremony was held, described by Coleman:

> When the maidens fair bade 'good-bye,' I asked them to pray for us; but one, more lively than the others, observed that we should be so much nearer heaven we ought to pray for them.

Coleman departed Whatcom in the company of Stratton, Ogilvy, their Indian boatman and Eldridge, who accompanied them for thirty miles before turning back. Bennett did not join them. The memory of the pain endured in the bivouac two years earlier was still strong, and he decided he preferred the amenities of the lowlands to high adventure. The party proceeded to the mouth of the Nooksack River, where they once again enlisted the skillful navigation services of Nooksack Indians and their "shovel-nosed canoes." Four Indians were to accompany them on the adventure; two, Squock and Talum, had been with Coleman on the earlier Nooksack River attempt.

Coleman and party portaging the canoes.

On August 7 they started up the river. When they reached the log jam, Coleman left the portaging to the Indians and again paid a visit to John Tennant. Despite Tennant's infirmities during the climb two years earlier, Coleman had been impressed with him. He asked Tennant to join the party, and Tennant again agreed. They returned to the canoes and continued up river. The water was high and going difficult in places. Another log jam required a portage. Poling through riffles was strenuous work, but they made good progress the first day and pitched camp for the night on the riverbank. Here Coleman discovered "defects in our culinary arrangement." He noted that the whole party had only one plate and spoon between them and wryly described the menu:

> Breakfast – Tea, bread, bacon.
> Dinner – Bread, bacon, tea.
> Supper – Bacon, tea, bread.

The intrepid group made do with what they had and got on their way early the next morning. They passed the last outpost of civilization, the homestead of a Colonel Patterson, and the village of the Nooksack Indians, and camped again. Continuing, they encountered forks in the river and chose to go up Nuxtig'um or the Middle Fork of the Nooksack. This would take them to the south of Mount Baker instead of up Cuwae-lic (North Fork), where Coleman had gone two years before. Squock and Talum recommended Nuxtig'um, "alleging that a day's journey would bring us to the head of navigation, and that in the three days' land travel between that and the snow line we would find occasional elk trails, and reach a point where the ascent was more easy." They struggled up the increasingly swift and shallow river assisted by a Nooksack Indian hunter, made three portages and poled through "twenty-seven riffles or rapids." These difficulties convinced them that camp that night would be the "head of navigation," so they cached their canoes and provisions, taking enough bacon, tea and bread for ten days. They set out on foot, hefting heavy packs, on August 11.

> . . .we plunged into the forest along the bank of the river in order to reach a ford some twelve miles up. With difficulty we made about a mile an hour, over fallen trees, under old logs, down steep ravines, over high rough rocks, and through close-set jungle.

The going was indeed difficult. Thick, almost impenetrable growths of vine maple required strenuous detours. Prickly spines of devil's club tore at them and frayed their tempers. According to Coleman, Stratton's high spirits carried them along, and they finally pitched "Camp Fatigue" on the river bank

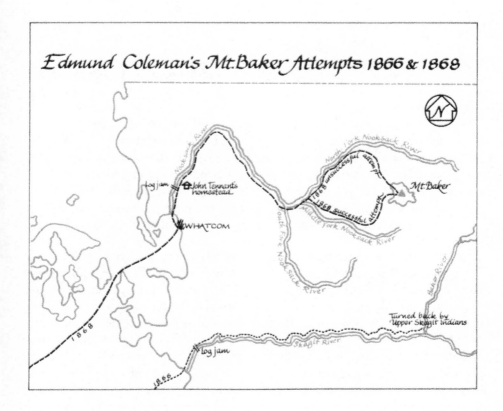

where the waters of what came to be knows as Clearwater Creek joined the larger stream.

Next morning they continued, encountering more difficult travel. Uncertainty increased their vexation; they were unsure where to turn uphill from the river toward the mountain. After a second exhausting day they pitched "Camp Doubtful" beside another roaring tributary of the river.

Squock and Talum were dispatched on a scouting mission next morning. Coleman got out his sketchbook, while Stratton, Tennant and Ogilvy went prospecting. The Indians returned late in the day with word that they had found a way up to snow line. They had also killed some marmots to supplement the expedition's monotonous diet. The prospectors had found no sign of gold. Despite the hopeful news, Coleman could not sleep:

> The expectation of five years' solitude and exile was about to be realized, or else delayed until another season had wearily come round. The struggle maintained in the land of the stranger approached it denouement. Was I to stand a conqueror upon the

mountain summit, or return with the memory of defeat to behold it from the shore of my island home.

He finally dropped off to sleep, but dreamed of dangers. Suddenly he started awake:

> My companions were sunk in sleep around me, the campfire had died out, the night was cold and chilly. The noise of the river, deafening during the day, was like thunder in the stillness of the night. The thought that it had thus fought its coarse [sic] night and day, throughout the rolling centuries, filled me with awe. It seemed like some remorseless being madly bent on destruction, and was to me an emblem of unrelenting power and inexorable will.

The following morning, August 14, the forests were enveloped in thick fog, but Coleman felt much better once he got moving uphill. They climbed up through forests of hemlock and fir and gained the top of the ridge which was, according to Coleman, about five yards broad. The fog drifted by, opening occasionally to reveal a glacier far below them to the northeast. Worn out, they camped again, calling this one "Camp Hope." They were at an elevation of about six thousand feet on Marmot Ridge. Burning with thirst, with no potable water near their camp, they sent the Indians off with all of their pots and pans to find some. While they waited for the water they "were cheered by observing that the clearing of the fog had revealed two magnificent rock peaks or 'aiguilles,' as they are termed in Switzerland, to which we gave the names of 'Lincoln' and 'Colfax.'" The Indians returned with some water they had found five hundred feet below camp. The men downed their bacon, tea and bread and turned in.

Fog continued to surround them the next day, the fifteenth, so they decided not to climb. Coleman stayed in camp and sketched while part of the group set out hunting to supplement the boring rations. Hoping for bear or elk, of which they saw sign on the ridge, they returned with several marmots. According to Coleman, Stratton concocted a stew which "was consumed with a relish which none but hungry mountaineers can experience." Stratton himself, in recalling the meal, was more restrained, noting that the marmots "were acceptable as a fresh meal, though not very palatable."[3]

When they awoke at dawn on the sixteenth fog lay in the valley below, but the mountains were clear. They could see the cone of Mount Baker, the Black Buttes and the Twin Sisters Range to the south. Coleman compared the latter peaks in shape and color to the "Aiguilles Rouges" of Chamonix in the French Alps. They broke Camp Hope and continued up the ridge, which

Coleman's party ascending the Middle Fork of the Nooksack.

gradually flattened out, and established their final camp at 7,054 feet, according to Coleman's aneroid barometer. It was only 9 a.m. but too late to climb. Coleman continued his sketching. Ogilvy went hunting and bagged a ptarmigan. Coleman notes that Tennant and Stratton

> . . . went to try some creepers [crampons] which had been made for the occasion, being doubtful that they would answer; they also reconnoitered the proposed route. They returned in high spirits . . . declaring that with the creepers they could walk up the slopes of snow as firmly as on a hillside.

The party organized for the next day's bid for the summit.

At 5 a.m. they set off with provisions for twenty-four hours. The weather was clear, their spirits high. By 6:30 a.m. they reached the end of the ridge, where the Indians bid them well and set off back to camp. The four climbers looked out across the glacier and immediately disagreed about the best route to their objective. Coleman was for following the ridge to the top of Colfax; his experience in the Alps had taught him that this was the safest way to go, along the ridge, whatever the difficulties (and there would be insurmountable difficulties on this ridge should they choose to go that way). Stratton, with "a happy ignorance of the dangers of concealed crevasses or chasms and the frailties of snow bridges," according to Coleman, set out on his own track right across the glacier below Lincoln Peak.

Coleman, Tennant and Ogilvy talked the situation over and decided to follow Stratton who was by now out of sight among the ridges and hummocks of the glacier. They roped up and set off, "in considerable anxiety concerning Stratton." Occasionally they caught a glimpse of him far ahead as they slowly made their way across the névé below Colfax Peak. Coleman was tired, has age telling on him by his account, but he plodded along. The three made their way to the saddle between Colfax Peak and the main peak without incident. Mounting a ridge of rotting volcanic debris, they looked down the southern side of the mountain. It was time for rest and refreshment:

> Ogilvy pounded some ice, and, with the aid of brandy, made a cocktail; it was very acceptable, and was christened the Mount Baker cocktail. Its fame reached Victoria, where it was reproduced at one of the bars; and, aided by the exhibition of a veritable piece of rock from the summit, attracted thirsty crowds . . . fortified by this refreshment and an hour's rest, we made for the top of the saddle by the northern side of these rocks.

A long ridge of "a deposit resembling mud" stretched above the saddle for several hundred feet upward toward what is known today as the Roman Wall. Its top is a flat, rocky bench; here they caught up with Stratton, who was feeling rather sickly due to the "sulphurous exhalations" issuing from the crater a short distance to the east. Despite his nausea he was ready for the final slope. Coleman describes the section that had frustrated him and Bennett two years earlier:

> Around the summit of the peak is a perpendicular wall of ice about thirty or forty feet in height, terminated on the left or northern end by a knuckle of rock, which can be plainly seen from the

Sound. The only passage we could discern through this barrier is on the left, between the knuckle of rock before-mentioned and the wall of ice. The face of the peak is scored with deep furrows, made by avalanches of ice which have fallen from the summit. The peak rises about 1000 feet higher. It commences with a gentle slope, and gradually becomes steeper, until near the summit it is about 60°.

They started up, encountering no problems at first, but as the slope steepened it became necessary to cut steps. Stratton was going strong again, so he took the lead.

The axe was passed on to Stratton, who plied it with vigor and skill. While thus engaged he got a great fright. Having heard a dull, grating sound, he looked up and saw a mass of frozen snow, about 12 feet square, moving down toward him. Paralyzed with terror, he was about to warn us, when it stopped. Even at this height there were crevasses. Into one of these Tennant sank, but managed to extricate himself.

They gained the knuckle of rock, rested there for a short time, and walked onto the summit plateau. It was 4 p.m. Coleman's dream was realized

The summit was white, with no rocks showing. The view was obscured by a pall of smoke from forest fires which "lay like a reddish cloud beneath us." Stratton describes the scene:

What an indescribable feeling passed over us! No word was spoken, as we stood with clasped hands, contemplating the majestic grandeur of the scene. At such a time and such a place one feels the spirit of inspiration that led the Psalmist to exclaim, "Great are Thy works, O Lord!"[4]

They sang an appropriate religious song, then planted the Stars and Stripes, and sang a patriotic song. A flask of brandy was produced, and everyone interested in the expedition was duly honored. Looking across the summit snow, Coleman saw a small peak on the far end. Wanting to be sure they were truly on the highest point of the mountain, they trudged across to it and duly planted the flag again. This bump on the northeast corner of the summit plateau was indeed the true summit.

Coleman sketched while the others looked around the summit. They found a vantage point where they could look into the crater. Stratton described their view as "an awful sight. Down, down – all dark and sulphury, with green, black, red and yellow sides."[5] Wisps of steam rose from vents in the crater. Though impressed with what they had seen, they did not tell Coleman of their discovery, presumably fearing he would want to sketch the scene although the hour was growing late. The sun was dropping rapidly in the west, and they "stood upon a little island, surrounded by a boundless sea of vapor."[6]

Coleman's sketching done, they roped up and set off on their descent, prompted by fears of being benighted on the mountain as Coleman and Bennett had been two years earlier. The steep upper section of the Roman Wall, the descent of which had been haunting them on the summit, proved easy; they walked and slid quickly down to their packs at the bottom of the wall. They left the summit at 6 p.m. and pressed downward. Coleman notes:

> The sun was already sinking, so we had no time to lose. Urged by the fear of having to pass the night on the mountain, we plunged after Stratton down the slopes, across snow-bridges, by walls of ice, as if pursued by a fiend. Vain were my remonstrances, fearful of an accident, but my companions hurried in a manner that would have sent a Swiss guide into fits. Such a helter-skelter mad-brained party was never seen on either Mont Blanc or Mont Rosa.

As darkness closed in around them, they lost their way and were forced to backtrack until they found their tracks of the morning ascent. Coleman was exhausted, but his younger companions urged him onward till at 9 p.m. they arrived at the point where they had left the ridge and taken to the snow. Two more hours of effort in the darkness finally brought them to their high camp, where the Indians had a large fire going and were anxiously awaiting them. Refreshed by bowls of tea, they turned in. Even as they did so, the wind began to rise and a storm moved in upon them. Coleman, in rare understatement, noted that "as we turned round in our blankets, we felt thankful that we were not on the mountain."

The next day was devoted to rest and sketching, and then they set out on the return journey. The date was August 19. Instead of retracing their steps, they decided to take advantage of the high open subalpine parklands as much as possible. The descended to the west along Grouse Ridge rather than down their ascent route on Marmot Ridge. One camp on the ridge and a long day brought them down Clearwater Creek and back to Camp Fatigue. The return canoe trip with the current of the Nooksack was fast and exciting, and by August 22 the group was back on Bellingham Bay, completing their two-week journey.

The first ascent of Mount Baker seems to have been the high point in

Coleman's depiction of climbing onto the summit plateau.

the life of Edmund T. Coleman.[7] He had come out from England for, among other reasons, adventure and satisfaction of his passion for mountains. He had come with artistic and perhaps even literary ambitions as well. Upon his return to Victoria he wrote a lengthy account of his Mount Baker adventures and sent it, along with his sketches, to one of the major publishing houses in New York. His article was published in *Harpers New Monthly Magazine*, one of the leading periodicals of the time, illustrated with woodcuts of his sketches. Coleman had advanced himself not only as a mountaineer, but also as an artist and writer.

Though there is no evidence that Coleman succeeded in any major mountaineering ventures after Mount Baker, he appears once more in North American mountaineering history. In August of 1870 Coleman joined two young men on what turned out to be generally credited as the first complete ascent of Mount Rainier. He was not, however, with Hazard Stevens and Philemon Van Trump when they reached the summit. Coleman was older and more cautious than his companions, fell behind on the difficult approach to the mountain, and never even made it to snow line. Stevens and Van Trump were unkind to Coleman in later descriptions of their adventures, and he was undoubtedly disappointed in this unhappy end to his climbing career.

After this fiasco Coleman continued his travels in the Pacific Northwest for several years. He visited Portland in 1871 and continued south to San Francisco. In 1873 he traveled to Chicago on the newly completed Union Pacific Railroad and eastward home to England. Little is known of his life there, but he published articles about his travels and explorations in the American West and continued writing about mountains. Coleman died in London on May 24, 1892, at the age of 68.

2

Early History of the Mount Baker Region

Farthest away in the west, as near the western sea as mountains can stand, are the Cascades . . . . Kulshan, misnamed Mount Baker by the vulgar, is their northernmost buttress up at 49 and Frazer's River. Kulshan is an irregular, massive, mount-shaped peak, worthy to stand a white emblem of perpetual peace between us and our brother Britons.

– Theodore Winthrop, 1862

The first humans to have any contact with Mount Baker were the Indians who lived in sight of it. Many of them undoubtedly gazed up at it from their lowland home sites. The Lummis, for instance, lived in the San Juan Islands; on clear days the mountain dominates the eastern view from these islands. Few Indians ventured onto the slopes of the mountain itself, though the Nooksacks who lived to the west of its base, and the Upper Skagits to the south and east, hunted game and gathered berries in its forests and subalpine meadows. There is no evidence that Indians walked the glaciers or climbed the mountain.

How long were the Indians in the vicinity of Mount Baker? The archaeological record is not conclusive, but it seems to indicate that Indians first lived in the Puget lowlands some eleven to twelve thousand years ago. They may well have ventured into the highlands soon after they arrived in the area.[1] They lived in the upper Skagit region and perhaps along the Nooksack as well. Inhabiting the region continuously up to historic times, they gradually increased their ability to use the rich resources of their environment. Coastal groups based their hunting and gathering lifestyle on sea mammals and salmon, while inland groups like the Nooksack and Upper Skagit hunted big game like deer, elk and mountain goat and fished the rivers for salmon.[2]

33

Pursuit of the mountain goat probably brought the Nooksack and Skagit Indians closest to Mount Baker. They undoubtedly ate goat meat, but the goat's most important product was its hair, long and thick, great for winter warmth. The Indians gathered this "wool" to weave their Salish-style blankets. It was not always necessary to kill the goat to get its wool; in spring and early summer the goats shed their wool in great clumps, leaving it hanging on bushes or simply lying in tufts on the huckleberry bushes in alpine meadows. Perhaps they thrash around in the brush intentionally to rid themselves of their overly warm winter coats. Goats have predictable movement patterns, so the wool could be found in the same general areas every year. The Nooksacks and Upper Skagits probably knew well the goat paths and the likeliest shedding areas. True, they killed the goats for their meat and hides when they could, but they also simply gathered the hair from these areas. Either hunting or gathering wool would have brought the Indians to timberline in places with full view of Mount Baker's upper slopes.

Goat wool was important to upriver Indians, for it gave them something to exchange with lowland tribes, who valued warm blankets but had no direct access to the goats. The Nooksacks and Upper Skagits could trade their wool for marine mammal products to which they in turn had no access. The Nooksacks jealously protected their goat-hunting grounds, which explains the anger of Edmund Coleman's Indian guides in 1868 upon discovering evidence of Indian "poaching" game on Marmot Ridge, southeast of the mountain. The guides thought the poachers were probably Thompson Indians from British Columbia; two years earlier a Thompson had been killed by a Nooksack hunter for poaching in that area. Because Skagit Indians also hunted goats on Mount Baker, precise territorial hunting lines must have been established.

Indian groups had different names for the mountain. Early settlers thought the Lummis referred to it as *Koma Kulshan*, which has been variously translated. Charles Buchanan, writing around 1913, mentions that:

> Kulshan is a Lummi word indicating that the summit of the peak has been damaged, or blown off by an explosion ("just as if shot at the end," as one Indian explained it). This word is used of other things damaged or supposed to be damaged in a similar manner, and it is not limited at all in its use to Mt. Baker. The term does not mean "The Great White Watcher," or "The Shining One," as commonly interpreted.[3]

Linguistic research offers another explanation for the origin of the name Koma Kulshan. The source of *Kulshan* may be the Nooksack *kweles*, "to shoot." Incorporated into a phrase description of a common hunting practice, it would have been *kwomae kwelsaen,* meaning "go up high or way back in the mountains shooting." The proper Nooksack name for the peak was *kweq smaenit,* which is translated as "white mountain."[4] Early settlers struggling to understand Indian languages adopted the phrase *kwomae klelsaen* as the proper name and, perhaps not accurately distinguishing Indian names for the mountain and the region around it, accepted Koma Kulshan as the Indian name for the peak.

The Upper Skagits referred to the volcano as *t'kuba,* meaning "snow all around." The mountain was one of their guardian spirits, one reputed supplier of the berries that grew abundantly on its slopes.[5] Such spirits were "owned" by members of the Upper Skagit community and brought various attributes to their owners. There is no record of what attributes *t'kuba* brought to its owners, who acquired it through a prescribed quest in their youth.[6] The guardian spirits spent most of the year with others of their kind, according to the Skagits, in a world outside the human one. They would come on particular occasions when their human owners needed help, and at least once each year, when a special ceremony was held for them. This spirit world was central to the traditional religion of the people who lived close to the mountain, though the mountain spirit itself does not seem to have been of unusual stature or significance.

Aboriginal people of the Northwest Coast and elsewhere often developed stories and myths to explain the world around them. Charles Buchanan recorded one such story, a Lummi tale explaining the origin of Mounts Baker and Rainier and other familiar geographic features.

> In the olden days, so the old folks tell us, Kulshan was a fair and handsome youth who grew apace to man's estate and then espoused two wives. One of these wives fully equaled her husband in beauty – she was the favorite wife and her name was Duh-hwähk. She bore Kulshan three fine sons. The other wife was no match for Duh-hwähk in beauty but she was very amiable, very kind, and very attractive in manner. This wife was named Whäht-kwäy. Eventually it came about that the kindness and consideration of Whäht-kwäy so completely won over her husband that she supplanted Duh-hwähk in the affections of Kulshan. This, of course, aroused furious fires of jealousy and resentment in the breast of Duh-hwähk, who constantly kept the entire household in dissension and strife by means of her temper and her jealousy. Finally Duh-hwähk resolved to regain Kulshan by artifice. Relying confidently on her beauty and on her former firm sway over her hus-

band she conceived the plan of feigning to desert him.

So, one day, when it happened that by chance she found Kulshan in an amiable and mellow mood and more pliant to her purpose, she complained to him of the coldness and harshness which she, Duh-hwähk, had been treated in the household, even more by Whäht-kwāy than by Kulshan. She assured her husband that she loved him but that the burden was more than even her great love for him could bear and that unless he soon changed these conditions she must leave him and take with her all of her possessions. Kulshan resolved to be master in his own household and without hesitation informed Duh-hwähk that she could go as soon as she chose and as far as she liked. Duh-hwähk was dumfounded by this unexpected reply. She felt that she must make things appear to him in a more serious light. She felt confident in his love and sure that at the last Kulshan would relent. Indeed, she could not believe that he would really permit her thus to desert him. Founding her faith on this imagination she gathered her possessions and made ready to go at once. She prepared her pack thoroughly, putting therein plentiful supplies of berries, fruit, sweet bulbs, and even beautiful flowering plants of many varieties. Thus amply provided with all that she desired she then said farewell and fared forth, leaving her three children behind. The children bewailed the going of their mother and with many lamentations besought her to remain. This greatly pleased Duh-hwähk at heart for she now felt assured of melting the indifference of Kulshan. She was sure that he would call her back before she had been able to go any very great distance.

With this in mind she managed to set forth on a course that would take her the longest way. So also she traveled down the valley between the mountain ranges so as to be always in sight of Kulshan as long as possible, thinking to give him ample opportunity to recall her. She had not gone far, however, before she realized her mistake and richly repented her hasty action. So, as she went along, she would ever and anon look anxiously back. Her heart surged tumultuously with the fond hoping and the vain longing to see Kulshan wildly signal for her return – how she hoped that he would do so! Alas, she had gone too far for that, perhaps, and, besides, many little hills and valleys now intervened between her and home where she had left Kulshan and the weeping children. Therefore, she must needs climb the knolls and pick out the highest hills from which to gaze back with longing eyes and sinking heart. Standing on the very summits of these hills she would strain with all her might, up to the very tips of her toes, seeking some sign from her loved husband. Sometimes she fancied she was not quite high enough and she would raise to her tip-toes, and stretch forth her head in anxious gaze, yearning all the while and striving all the while to be just a little taller. This oft-repeated wish and effort soon began to have its effect upon her and she forthwith began to grow taller. At last she had gone so far that she must of necessity make camp. She selected as her stopping place one that seemed most satisfactory to her because from it she could have a clear view of her dear home so foolishly and uselessly abandoned. Here she removed her packs and cast the contents broadcast, blessing the place with all the stores of fruit, of berries, bulbs, tubers, and beautiful flowering plants of many wonderful varieties, all of which she had taken away from Kulshan. There, looking ever and longingly northward, Duh-hwähk remains to this day and you may see her if you wish – look to the south and east – it is Mount Rainier where Duh-hwähk cast them forth before she herself became the mountain. To the north lies the deserted husband, Kulshan, robbed of fruits and the beautiful things which Duh-hwähk took with her. Look to the north and you will see him, but the white man calls him Mount Baker, not Kulshan! All about Kulshan, too, you may see the deserted and weeping children.[7]

There were powerful spirits in the mountains, which is perhaps why Indians seemed not to have ventured high onto the glaciers of Mount Baker. When Stevens and Van Trump enlisted their Indian guide, Sliuskin, to help them climb Mount Rainier, he would reportedly not go beyond snow line. "In the lake lives a mighty demon. If you should reach the top, the demon will seize you and kill you and throw you into the fiery lake."[8] He expressed amazement when, two days after leaving him, Stevens and Van Trump returned and reported they had been to Rainier's summit. Similarly Squock and Talum would not venture onto the snows with Edmund Coleman. Perhaps they understood the risk of hidden crevasses thanks to sad experiences of their forebears and saw no reason to venture onto the glacier. Some Indians reported Mount Baker to have a fiery and dangerous aspect:

Kulshan once got so mad that a big piece fell off and slid away down the mountain. This made a big fire and lots of noise. Kulshan and Shuksan became black all over. The waters in the rivers became black and warm. Fish came floating down the rivers cooked. Lots of Indians and animals fled. Next year most of them went back again. Since then Kulshan has never been mad.[9]

This might well have been an account of a volcanic eruption of the mountain.

Mount Baker also appears in a legend of the Squamish, an Indian group that lived along Howe Sound, in British Columbia, not far to the north. The mountain is central to their account of the great flood or deluge, stories of which have been found in the traditions of many Pacific Northwest Indian groups. Faced with the prospect of the flood, Squamish men built a giant canoe, and women wove a strong rope with which to anchor it. They fastened the rope to the canoe and to a large rock and placed their babies and young children in the boat, along with food and fresh water for many days. The mother of the youngest baby and the bravest young man also embarked as guardians of the children.

As the floodwaters rose, the rest of the group was drowned, but the canoe safely rode the rising waters for many days. Then, as the rain subsided and the waters began to fall, the man saw land. It was the summit of Mount Baker. Cutting the anchor rope, they paddled to the mountain and landed on its flanks.

When the waters had gone down and the land below was dry, they made a new camp. They built their lodges in the region between the Fraser River and the Georgia Strait, in sight of Mount Baker. The children lived and grew up. Through them the Squamish people were saved.[10]

Indians lived with Mount Baker for thousands of years before white people appeared on the scene. With their passion for "discoverers," white students of the mountain's history have speculated about who might have been the first white person to see it. Charles Finley Easton, a long-time student of the mountain and the first historian of the Mount Baker Club, expended much energy on the question. He drew an elaborate map and located on it what he called the "theoretic horizon" from which an early explorer might have been able to see the mountain in good weather. Beyond that horizon the curvature of the earth would have made seeing it impossible, no matter the weather. Then he plotted the courses of the explorers who sailed the Northwest Coast and might have seen the mountain.[11]

The earliest visitors to the Northwest coastal waters seem to have sailed waters beyond Easton's theoretic horizon for they made no record of a volcano on land to the east. The Russians, who established themselves in the Aleutian Islands in the mid-eighteenth century, were working their way along the coast in search of furs. To the south, the Spanish had occupied Mexico and explored northward to San Francisco Bay. Perceiving that the Russians might thwart their territorial ambitions, the Spanish dispatched an expedition in 1773 to establish their dominion along the Northwest Coast up to 60° north latitude. Juan Perez reached the vicinity of the Queen Charlotte Islands but was forced to turn back southward by the onset of scurvy in his crew. At 49°30' north latitude he found a protected harbor and anchored in what is thought to have been Nootka Sound on the west coast of Vancouver Island.

The next year, another Spanish expedition was dispatched from San Blas, Mexico. Under the command of Bruno de Heceta, and accompanied by Bodega y Quadra, the expedition was to sail to 65° north latitude, then explore southward and take possession of the coast for Spain. They anchored off the coast of present-day Washington, and landing parties went ashore to take possession. Seven members of one of the parties were killed by Indians, probably at Moclips, an inauspicious start for these, the first white men known to stand on the shores of Washington. Heceta sailed south after this incident and returned to his base in Mexico. None of the Russians or Spanish recorded sighting any volcanoes on their eastern horizon.

A few years later, Captain James Cook of the Royal Navy sailed up the coast and landed at Nootka Sound. Bad weather had prevented him from sighting the Strait of Juan de Fuca, but his visit to the Northwest Coast was significant – it brought England into the region. Though Cook was killed the next winter by natives in Hawaii, his ship continued exploration of the Alaska Coast and proceeded to China, where the immense value of the furs the crew had collected along the Pacific Northwest Coast became evident. Furs would provide the incentive for much future British activity in the region.

Word spread about these rich fur resources; English and American traders and sailors appeared. In July of 1787 the English maritime trader William Barkley sighted the entrance to a great inlet, the Strait of Juan de Fuca. Its presence was also noted by an American trader, Robert Gray, but neither of them ventured very far into the strait. The British trader Captain John Meares also sighted the strait in 1788 and named it for the Greek Apostolus Valerianos, also known as Juan de Fuca, whom he thought had been the first European to visit the strait in 1596. The likelihood that any of these earliest explorers penetrated Easton's theoretic horizon and saw Mount Baker is slight, but they were laying the groundwork for those who soon would spot the peak.

The mountain was first recorded by a European in 1790. The Spanish had established a settlement at Nootka in 1789, and when word of the existence of the strait reached Spanish officials, they sent an expedition to chart it. Ensign Manuel Quimper of the Spanish Navy was in charge; his first

Charles Easton's drawing of Mount Baker.

pilot was Gonzalo Lopez de Haro. Quimper's sloop probed its way along the north shore of the strait to the present site of Victoria, British Columbia, from which the mountain is visible on a clear day. The party crossed the strait to Dungeness Bay. Quimper's second pilot, Juan Carrasco, took his longboat eastward and sighted Rosario Strait and Deception Pass. After a few days charting Dungeness Bay, Quimper proceeded out of the strait, crossing first to the southern shore of Vancouver Island, then coming back south in search of fresh water. He made the first explorations of the north coast of the Olympic Peninsula.[12] In the course of all this Quimper and his party spent weeks in places where Mount Baker would be visible to them. Though Quimper made no reference to the mountain in his journal of the voyage, Haro's manuscript chart of Strait of Juan de Fuca includes a sketch of a prominent peak in the Mount Baker region titled "La Gran Montana del Carmelo."[13] Thus was Mount Baker "discovered."

Another Spanish party came through the strait in June of 1791 under the leadership of Juan Francisco de Eliza. They explored the San Juan Islands to the Strait of Georgia and probably saw the mountain, for they spent the full month of July in view of it. They encountered Indians on Padilla Bay and Point Roberts, who told them that other white men had preceded them in large ships and even over land. Eliza's party recorded nothing about Mount Baker.

Spain had sent two vessels into Nootka in 1789 to fortify and protect the harbor, still trying to retain their claim to dominion over the region. In trying to protect the harbor, they created an international incident by seizing ships flying the English flag. This event ultimately led to a treaty signed in Madrid in 1790 between Spain and England called the Nootka Convention. In the treaty Spain conceded to England that she could trade anywhere on the Pacific Coast north of the forty-second parallel, the current boundary between Oregon and California. England could also set up posts and set-tlements anywhere that Spain had not already occupied. Finally, reparations would be made for English ships and other property taken at Nootka. In 1791 the British Admiralty commissioned George Vancouver as commander of an expedition to survey the Northwest Coast and to proceed to Nootka to meet with the Spanish representative there for the purpose of carrying out the terms of the Nootka Convention.

Vancouver left England on April 1, 1791, with two ships, H.M.S. *Discovery* and H.M.S. *Chatham*. They passed around the Cape of Good Hope to southwestern Australia, New Zealand, Tahiti, and then to the Hawaiian Islands, where they spent the winter. On March 16, 1792, they sailed for the Pacific Northwest, arriving on the coast of Washington on April 28. There they met the American fur-trading ship *Columbia* commanded by Robert Gray. Vancouver learned what he could from Gray about the Strait of Juan de Fuca, sailed into the strait with a gentle wind and clear weather and made for Dungeness Bay, on the south shore of the strait, Quimper's anchorage two years earlier. At about 5 p.m. Third-lieutenant Joseph Baker, on board the *Discovery*, happened to look to the northeast:

> About this time a very high conspicuous craggy mountain, bearing by compass N.50E. presented itself, towering above the clouds: as low down as they allowed it to be visible it was covered with snow; and south of it, was a long ridge of very rugged snowy mountains, much less elevated, which seemed to stretch to a considerable dis-tance . . . .the high distant land formed, as already observed, like detached islands, amongst which the lofty mountain, discovered in the afternoon by the third lieutenant, and in compliment to him called by me MOUNT BAKER, rose a very conspicuous object, bearing by compass N.43E., apparently at a very remote distance.[14]

Thus, though Haro had named the mountain on his chart in 1790, it fell to an Englishman to give the peak the name it bears today. Haro's chart went unpublished for eighty-two years, by which time the Spanish had long been gone from the region. In the official narrative of Vancouver's voyage, print-ed in London in 1798, there appears the first published reference to Mount Baker.

The man for whom the mountain was named remains a rather obscure figure. Third-lieutenant Baker was from an old Norman family of Bristol, England. His father, Captain Valentine Baker, had enjoyed a distinguished Royal Navy career, from which he had retired to become Harbor Master at Bristol. Joseph was his fourth surviving son and aspired to follow his father in a naval career. Captain Vancouver was very impressed with the young man and eventually gave him command of the *Discovery*. Baker eventually became a captain and died in Bristol in 1817.

Mount Baker was one of George Vancouver's first "discoveries" on his voyage to the Northwest. His ships lay over at Port Discovery for sixteen days for refitting and repairs; Vancouver and some of his men explored southward and eastward during this period. On May 18 the *Chatham* explored northward, and the *Discovery* entered Admiralty Inlet. The two ships commenced thirty-eight days of exploration of what Vancouver named Puget Sound (after another of his lieutenants, Peter Puget). In the course of these explorations the party observed another large mountain to the south and east; Vancouver named it Mount Rainier. His explorations in the area completed, Vancouver sailed north on June 24 and accomplished the first recorded circumnavigation of Vancouver Island. Native American war canoes had raided southward to the Olympic Peninsula from as far north as the Queen Charlotte Islands, so they may have routinely circumnavigated this huge island, but of course they did not record their voyages as the European explorers were doing. Vancouver anchored at Nootka Sound where, according to plan, he met with Bodega y Quadra regarding the Nootka Convention. Vancouver and Quadra could not reach agreement as to how the terms of the convention were to be carried out, but other negotiators three years later did so, resulting in Spanish abandonment of Nootka. Thenceforth the Spanish were to play no role in the history of the Mount Baker region.

Mount Baker had been discovered, recorded and named but was not to figure centrally in the lives of Americans and Europeans for seventy-four years. During this time the United States and England wrangled over who should possess that part of North America north of the Columbia River. The English hoped to control all land south to the River, and American aspirations extended as far north as 54°40' north latitude – nearly to the current southeast Alaska. After a period of joint occupancy during which the present state of Washington was controlled by the North West Company and then the Hudson's Bay Company (the two merged in 1821), the Mount Baker region became American in 1846. England decided that the country between the Columbia and Fraser Rivers was not worth a war with the United States. The fur resources of the region were declining and the Hudson's Bay Company purposely sought to exhaust them in an effort to deny them to rival Americans. Having depleted the furs in the Columbia River system, the Company agreed to move its western headquarters from Fort Vancouver on the Columbia River to Vancouver Island, at the present site of Victoria. After much negotiation the forty-ninth parallel was agreed upon as the international boundary, beginning at the Rocky Mountains and running due west to the

An Easton sketch of Lieutenant Joseph Baker and George Vancouver's ship, the Discovery.

center of the channel separating Vancouver Island from the continent, then following the center of that channel southerly, bisecting the Strait of Juan de Fuca to the Pacific Ocean. There would be minor disputes, but the central territorial question was resolved. Settlement on both sides of the border could proceed.

No evidence can be found of any special interest in Mount Baker from its naming until Edmund Coleman began planning to climb it in the 1860s. During the first half of the century fur traders and trappers undoubtedly viewed the mountain, but they seldom kept records of their explorations; no reference to Mount Baker by such men is known. They traveled the Fraser River (beginning with Simon Fraser in 1808) and sailed among the San Juan Islands, but the rugged country surrounding Mount Baker did not attract them. Indians brought furs from near the mountain to Hudson Bay's Fort Langley, established in 1825 on the Fraser River, or to Fort Victoria after 1843. Some Skagit Indians even traded furs as far away as the Company's Nisqually House, established near present-day Olympia in 1833.[15]

The lowlands west of Mount Baker began to be settled at mid-century, after establishment of the international boundary. In 1850, Isaac Ebey came to Whidbey Island and became the first permanent settler in lower Skagit territory. Captain Henry Roeder and Russell Peabody became the first settlers on Bellingham Bay late in 1852. In 1849 there were only 304 white people in Oregon Territory north of the Columbia River, but soon thereafter gold seekers disappointed in California came north – the 1850 census showed an increase to over one thousand people.[16] By 1853 there were enough settlers and enough political justification to warrant creation of a separate Washington Territory. By 1855 the pressures of settlement were sufficient to motivate the territorial government to seek a treaty with the Indians. In the infamous Point Elliot Treaty, representatives from many Puget Sound Indians groups (excluding the Nooksacks, among others) ceded their land in return for reservations and other benefits. This treaty was to cause great trouble for the Indians around Mount Baker, but of course helped the process of white settlement.

The largest white community in the region was Fort Victoria on Vancouver Island. From this base the English sought to colonize what was to become the province of British Columbia, to insure that it remained English and did not go the way of the Columbia River country. For various reasons, settlement north of the international boundary, except at Victoria, was slow until the late 1850s. Before the Fraser River gold rush of 1858, the population of Victoria was approximately five hundred, mostly Hudson Bay Company employees, past and present, and their families.[17]

The white population of the Puget Sound lowlands near the mountain grew slowly during the 1850s. Coal mines opened at Sehome (now part of Bellingham) and provided employment as there was a lucrative coal market in San Francisco. Indian trouble on Bellingham Bay and throughout Washington Territory led to the establishment of Fort Bellingham in 1856. In August of that year, sixty-eight soldiers commanded by Captain George E. Pickett, later to achieve fame as a Confederate army general, arrived in Bellingham.

The greatest boost to settlement was the Fraser River gold rush of 1858. In February of 1858 the Hudson's Bay Company shipped eight hundred ounces of Fraser River gold dust to the United States Mint in San Francisco. Word got out, and thousands of stampeders came to Bellingham Bay and other places with access to the gold-producing river country. A rough trail running north from the village of Whatcom on the bay, long used by Indians trading in the Fraser River valley, was touted as the easiest way to the strike. The gold soon petered out, and the Whatcom Trail did not turn out to be such an easy route. Frustrated gold seekers began to filter back into Washington Territory, their hopes for riches dashed. Some went to work in the Sehome coal mines and eventually helped settle the Bellingham Bay and Nooksack River areas.

One recorded venture into the Mount Baker region during this period is that of the Northwest Boundary Survey, a party of English and American surveyors who set out to establish the precise location of the international boundary in 1858. While surveyors took their readings and laborers cut a swath through the forests and over mountainous terrain to mark the boundary, American topographer Henry Custer explored the country on both sides of the line. Custer, his survey companions, and his Indian guides ranged between the Fraser an Nooksack rivers, climbing peaks and exploring valleys. One foray took them through the low pass between what is now called Columbia Valley and Silver Lake, then down the outlet stream of the lake to the Nooksack River. Turning up river they passed the confluence of the North Fork of the Nooksack and Glacier Creek, the site of the modern community of Glacier, just a few miles from Mount Baker. Continuing on, they traveled up the North Fork to where it is joined by Ruth Creek, then followed this to its head at Hannegan Pass. An Indian trail, presumably one used by the Nooksacks for berrying and hunting, made travel up the river a straightforward venture. Custer saw Mount Baker on some of his climbs. He knew he was near it on his trip up the Nooksack River but had neither the time nor the means to attempt climbing it.

A second foray close to the mountain was that of the Tennant-Lane Expedition of 1860. Two of its five members were John Tennant and John Bennett, who would later return to the upper Nooksack with Edmund T. Coleman to attempt to climb Mount Baker. The 1860 group had no interest in the mountain, but was after gold. From Bellingham Bay they made their way to Lake Whatcom, then rafted up the lake and climbed over the pass to the east and into the valley of the South Fork of the Nooksack. Panning the river bars, they found some color, so hopefully but with difficulty, they made their way upstream. In the end they found little gold and returned discouraged. The most significant outcome of their expedition was that Tennant and Bennett became interested in the upper Nooksack region and learned something about it. They also met some of the Nooksack Indians who lived there, and were on good terms with them. Eight years later, when Coleman arrived at the growing community on Bellingham Bay and inquired about companions to accompany him, Tennant and Bennett would be mentioned and eventually agree to go on Coleman's historic adventure.

3

Prospectors and Pioneers

Many and wonderful have been the changes which have taken place beneath the shadow of our beloved snow-capped mountain – our Mount Baker, whose lofty peaks were seen but dimly through the towering branches of the giant trees which lined our rivers and filled our valleys at the time of which I write.
– Robert Emmett Hawley
Nooksack Valley Pioneer, 1945[1]

Edmund Coleman was an anomaly in the Washington Territory. An educated, urbane, esthetic gentleman, a painter – he was obsessed with climbing mountains, and particularly Mount Baker, merely for the sake of the climb and the pleasures of mountaineering. No others with this obsession appeared in the Mount Baker region for many years after his pioneering climb. Twenty three years would pass before the next climber stood atop the peak.

Events in the surrounding lowlands during this period made the mountain accessible to the next generation of mountaineers. Settlers slowly moved up the Nooksack and Skagit River valleys. They first established themselves at Mount Vernon on the Skagit in 1870; by 1877 logging had begun and settlers had moved as far upriver as Hamilton, due south of the mountain, to mine coal. In the Nooksack Valley settlers were moving on to the fertile and flat land along the river. By 1877 a road had been built from Whatcom on Bellingham Bay to Nooksack Crossing near the modern town of Everson. White settlers were in clear view of the mountain but had enough to do just to clear the great trees off their land so that they could plant and tend their crops. Settlers generally were family oriented, the men unwilling and uninterested in any unnecessary risks that might jeopardize the welfare of their families. They leaned occasionally on their shovels and axes to admire the view but made no move toward the mountain.

An early-century homestead, perched beside the Nooksack River.

Another breed still wandered the land, however, and these did venture into the hills. They sought not adventure but gold, though they usually found more adventure. In 1877 a party went up the Skagit River in search of gold, probed up the Baker River, found little there, and continued up the Skagit. They explored widely, panning in likely places, and by 1879 were washing payable quantities of gold out of creek gravels. Their success led to typically inflated stories of a bonanza at Ruby Creek on the Upper Skagit, and there was a bonafide rush there in 1879-80. Throngs of "Argonauts," as they were called in those days, estimated at more than a thousand, braved the hazards of the river and the mountains. Most were frustrated as usual and gained little from the great risks they took, but the Ruby Creek Mines, though many miles east of the mountain itself, proved to be an important stimulant to the opening of the Mount Baker region.

Gold rushers went up the Nooksack River into the Mount Baker region itself. No record exists of prospecting in the vicinity of the mountain after the Tennant-Lane expedition of 1860 until Thomas Barrett ventured into the

Pack train, loading up for a trip to the mines, early in 20th century.

South Fork Valley in 1878. Barrett, a gregarious fellow who kept the company store for the Sehome coal mines for many years, retired from storekeeping to try homesteading. Finding farm work a hard and rather lonesome grind, he returned to civilization, to Sehome, where he bought the coal company's saloon, which he knew had always been a lucrative business. What Barrett did not know when he bought the saloon was that the coal company was planning to shut down. When the mines closed, the would-be entrepreneur was broke. Like many others in similar straits, he decided to try to recover his losses by finding the gold rumored to be somewhere along the South Fork of the Nooksack. Pulling together an outfit with two companions, Barrett and associates explored, by his account, some one hundred miles of country up the South Fork. Barrett's luck remained poor; after six weeks of struggling with the rugged country south and west of Mount Baker, the seekers limped back into town, their clothes in tatters, their pockets empty. Barrett decided farm-

50

ing had its virtues after all and lived out his years on his farm with its modest but steady living.

Prospectors are like gamblers. Despite repeated frustration they remain eternally hopeful and cannot shake the lure of the strike. The rich bar may be just around the next bend in the creek, the mother lode in the mountains just upstream. Countless Tom Barretts went into the Mount Baker country with high hopes and returned in tatters. Argonauts were constantly probing into the hills. Two prospecting parties of the 1880s, though they found little gold, contributed significantly to the exploration of the mountain.

William Henry Dorr arrived in Whatcom County from Iowa in 1882 and established a homestead. One day he talked with a Nooksack Indian who claimed to have been hunting on Mount Baker's north side. According to Dorr, the Indian told him "that there was a place at the head of a stream of water a short distance below where it came out from under the snow over on that side of the mountain where it directly faces the rising sun in the long summer days, where there were heaps of gold."[2] The Indian knelt and drew a crude map in the sand. Dorr decided to investigate.

Carrying sixty-pound packs, Dorr and a friend set out for the mountain. They were guided by the Indian's map, which Dorr had copied from sand to paper. After four days of hard going up the North Fork, they reached the mouth of Glacier Creek. At times they had to walk in the riverbed to avoid the thick tangle of undergrowth along the bank. After a night's rest at the confluence of the two streams, they followed Glacier Creek for a mile, then climbed steeply uphill east of the creek to the top of Skyline Divide, which the Indian had said would provide a route to the region of the mountain where the gold was to be found.

They struck the ridgetop, a delightful place resplendent with flowering meadows and clumps of pointed firs. Up this ridge they went, after a pleasant camp among the flowers, from Skyline to Chowder Ridge, across a small glacier (Hadley Glacier) to a campsite on the north side of the slope where Cougar Divide meets Chowder Ridge. They knew they were close to their objective, for the mountain loomed just above them. Crossing Dobbs Creek, they walked to the very east end of Chowder Ridge and saw what must have been the site of the Indian's Eldorado, where Barr Creek emerged from beneath the Mazama Glacier.

> Here we located the Siwash gold mine. There was a sparkle of glittering mica about the edges of the water and mixed with finer grit in the eddies, just such a showing as might be expected to impress the untutored mind of the savage, but very disappointing to the prospector.[3]

Route of Dorr's 1880s summit attempt, as seen from Skyline Divide.

Still, they staked their claim, named it Siwash, and panned and explored the area. Their efforts went unrewarded, so they returned to their camp.

Perhaps Dorr looked up toward Mount Baker's summit and commented to his companion that since they had done better than half the work of climbing the mountain, they might as well go the rest of the way. The view would be good, and maybe it would even be fun. They set off up the northeast ridge, commonly known today as the Cockscomb Ridge.

> There was no bad climbing aside from the numerous broad and very deep crevasses but the rise was rapid being fully 30 per cent grade on the average. We reached a high point or spire of lava overlooking a steaming crater on this northeast slope but we were caught in a snow squall and forced to retrace our steps.[4]

The spire of lava is today called the Cockscomb, at approximately 9700 feet on the ridge. Good weather would not have assured them of success, for the spire is extremely crumbly volcanic rock and could not have been surmounted. With no climbing equipment or experience the pair could not have bypassed the rock on either side, for steep ice and crevasses make that a challenge even today.

They turned back, but left their mark on the mountain. The "steaming crater" they spotted below them was not a crater but a group of fumaroles. Today these are known as the Dorr Fumaroles, and plumes of steam can still sometimes be seen rising from them at the eight-thousand foot level.

Another party was on the mountain during the summer of 1884, this one on the opposite side from Dorr. They, too, were prospectors who went up the South Fork of the Nooksack. But according to L.L. Bales, who described the trip in an interview and article, they also intended to try to climb the mountain. Bales and four companions left Whatcom on June 16 and made their way to the South Fork, up which they traveled for a week. They went slowly, presumably looking for gold and exploring unfamiliar country. Bales broke out his fishing line from time to time, supplementing their trail food. He reported fishing to be excellent, even in the very upper reaches of the river. They climbed a minor peak of the Three Sisters group and eventually made their way to timberline on Baker's south side.

Three members of the party decided to climb, the other two to hunt mountain goats. The three climbers crossed a large glacier, which Bales refers to as the head of the Baker River, and "ascended the mountain from the southeast side."[5] One climber dropped out, and Bales and Victor Lowe continued upward. "After several hours of very difficult climbing, Mr. V.V. Lowe and myself succeeded in reaching the summit."[6] They enjoyed the view, then descended to their companions and returned to Whatcom by way of the Middle Fork of the Nooksack.

Victor Lowe

But did they make the summit of Mount Baker, as Bales led the readers of his 1890 *Pacific Magazine"* to believe? One student of the mountain's history, Harry Majors, credits Bales and Lowe with the second ascent, but there is reason to doubt.[7] An account of the climb was published in *The West Shore* in 1884, condensed from the account that appeared in the *Whatcom Reveille* shortly after the party returned from their adventure. In this account Bales and Lowe "persevered, and by constantly encouraging each other and resting every few steps, finally reached the apex of the eastern summit, about twenty-five feet lower than the dome-shaped summit visible from the Sound, and 150 yards distant from it. They were too exhausted by their efforts to attempt the other apex."[8] This "eastern summit" sounds suspiciously like Sherman Peak, which is approximately seven hundred feet below the actual summit and slightly over one-half mile away from it as the raven flies. Perhaps at this point the climbers exaggerated their closeness to the summit, though admit-

An Indian home in the Nooksack region.

ting that they had not made the last little bit to the top. Another more likely possibility given their description of their situation is that they emerged onto the summit plateau and gazed across to the small prominence on its northeast corner. Exhausted, they did not go this short additional distance. Either way they did not reach the summit.

There is also a descriptive detail in Bales' 1890 account that lends some credence to the Sherman Peak possibility. He says that he and his companions crossed "a large glacier, the head of Baker River, and ascended the mountain from the southeast side."[9] If the party came up the moraine known as Railroad Grade, crossed Easton Glacier to Squok Glacier, then struck for the highest point above them, they could have inadvertently found themselves atop Sherman Peak. If visibility was poor, as it often is, they might have climbed Sherman Peak thinking that they were on their way to the summit, only to gaze exhaustedly across at the higher peak from the point they had achieved. They were not at the "head" of the Baker River, but could credibly have thought the creek roaring out from under the Easton Glacier and draining toward the lake to have been the source of the river.

A 1906 article in the Seattle *Post-Intelligencer* lends some credence to the argument that Bales and Lowe were atop Sherman Peak rather than Mount Baker itself. Frank Teck, in reviewing climbs of Mount Baker, notes that "Lowe and Bales claimed they had reached the summit of Sherman Peak June 29, and discovered an immense extinct crater, a thousand feet deep and half a mile in diameter. . . ."[10] Thus Bales and Lowe probably made the first ascent of Sherman Peak, the pointed summit of the east rim of the crater. For whatever reason, Bales made an erroneous claim to the second ascent of Mount Baker in his 1890 account.

Sixteen years after Coleman's party made footprints across the summit plateau, several parties had followed new routes to the mountain's summit region. The lure of gold drew them to the area, but once they were close to the mountain it cast its own spell upon them. They responded to the challenge. The 1884 achievements were a sign of adventures and adventurers to come.

Another seven years were to pass before Mount Baker's summit snows were to beckon, but meanwhile events were unfolding that would make the mountain more accessible and clear the way for successful future ascents. Central to this part of the story are the Ruby Creek mines on the upper Skagit River mentioned earlier. When the gold rush up the Skagit was peaking, the economy of young communities on Bellingham Bay was in need of stimulation, and the idea for a road from Bellingham Bay to the mines was conceived. Entrepreneurs pushing for the road reasoned that it would bring mine-related business to their community. When the idea surfaced in 1879, there was no road beyond the Nooksack River at Nooksack Crossing, a few miles from the Bay, but that was no deterrent to boosters.

For several years there was much talk of the road but no action on the idea. Then in 1886 a party of six men traveled much of the route that road promoters were touting. One member of the party was Banning Austin, who was to figure prominently in later road developments. Austin's group left Whatcom on July 12 in search of a new route from Whatcom through the upper Skagit and "to do some prospecting for a mining and milling company."[11] Their route took them up the North Fork to Wells Creek, then up this creek until they could ascend a peak bordering the stream, probably Barometer Mountain or a promontory on Lasiocarpa Ridge. Their travels from there are uncertain, but somehow they made their way back to the Nooksack upstream from where they had left it and then continued up the river to Ruth Creek. Austin's party eventually reached the Skagit River after twenty-eight arduous days of travel

Great Excelsior Stamp Mill.

Banning Austin's fanciful map of the proposed road to the Ruby Creek Mines. The map failed to include the rugged Picket Range.

over extremely rough terrain. They had experienced the country that any road from Bellingham Bay to Ruby Creek mines would have to traverse. Given the difficulties of their travels and the obstacles encountered, one might expect that their report on the feasibility of building a road over their route would be discouraging but it was not.

Years passed after Austin's expedition, but the road idea remained strong in many minds. Slowly the trail up the Nooksack was made into a wagon road. By 1893 the road extended to the present site of Maple Falls. That year the Washington State Legislature, at the urging of local politicians, created State Road District Number One and provided twenty thousand dollars for the work, with other money to be contributed by the counties involved. The act provided for a state road through the Cascade Mountains north of Mount Baker to connect eastern and western Washington. The road was to go up the Nooksack River north of Mount Baker to a point on the Columbia River opposite the town of Marcus in Stevens County.

Banning Austin was hired to survey the route, since he called himself an engineer and knew the country as well as anyone. Austin, E.P. Chace, H. Hall and R. Lyle went up the North Fork to the boggy area called Breckenridge Bottoms, just downriver from the mouth of Ruth Creek. They could see a low pass to the south, west of Mount Shuksan. Austin, perhaps remembering the eastward jumble of mountains from his earlier foray, decided to investigate this pass, hoping for an alternative. The pass, which came to be called Austin Pass, proved discouraging, so they returned to the river. Replenishing their supplies, they climbed up Ruth Creek again to Hannegan Pass (named for one of the road commissioners, T.F. Hannegan). Dropping to the Chilliwack River, they went downstream to Brush Creek, then up Brush Creek to Whatcom Pass. Continuing, they traveled down Little Beaver Creek, then climbed a ridge from which they could look down the valley of Big Beaver Creek. Convinced they had found a feasible route, they returned to Whatcom with enthusiastic reports.

Construction began immediately. During 1893 road work reached six miles above Nooksack Falls, and the trail was improved to within a few miles of Hannegan Pass. As the summer passed, problems with finances and authority reared up, resulting in the resignation of two the road commissioners. A new commission was appointed and a new reconnaissance launched. The utter futility of trying to build a road over the proposed route to the Ruby Creek mines and Eastern Washington over the tortuous topography of the proposed route was finally recognized and the project was scrapped. By this time the Ruby Creek mines were of no great commercial importance and business minds on Bellingham Bay had new schemes for improving their economy, most of which involved railroads.

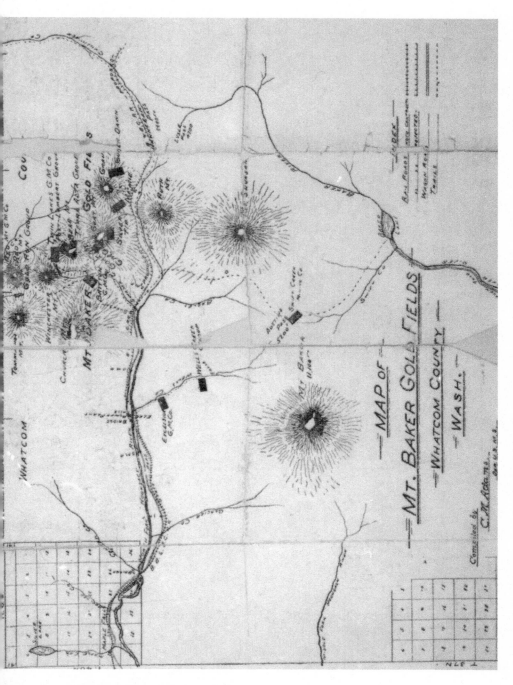

Gold fields map of 1902 mining heyday.

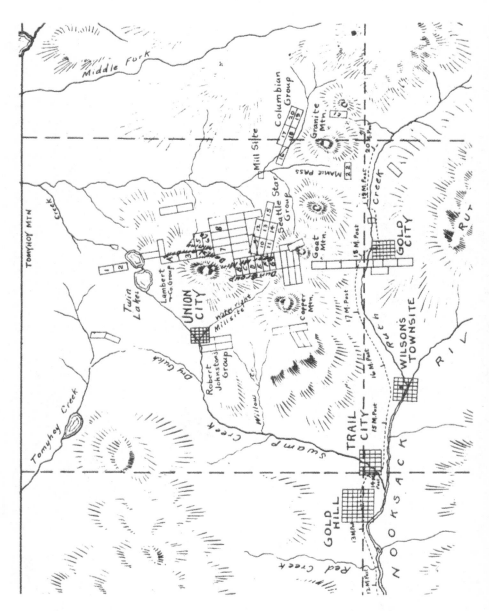

Late nineteen-century map showing claims and townsites in the Twin Lakes area during the peak of prospecting activity.

The North Cascades road fiasco provided the impetus for road building well up the valley of the North Fork of the Nooksack River, thereby considerably improving access to the Mount Baker region. After 1893 it was easier to get to the mountain, and even more prospectors and mountaineers began traveling into the region. A cross-Cascades road was ultimately built, but the idea hatched in 1879 did not come to fruition until 1972 with the opening of the North Cascades Highway which, ironically, went up the Skagit River instead of the Nooksack.[12]

While this wildly impractical road building scheme was occupying some people, others were quietly going about the business of settling the country around the mountain. The first settler moved into the valley of the South Fork in 1883, and others soon followed. A town site called Livewood was laid out at the mouth of Skookum Creek in 1885. Rumors of gold found in the area led to a minor rush of cheechacos and sourdoughs, as newcomers and oldtimers in the prospecting business were respectively called. *The Reveille*, a paper which had recently started publishing in Whatcom, ran the headline, "RICH MINES ABSOLUTELY FOUND ON THE SOUTH FORK OF THE NOOKSACK!!" The editor wrote:

> Now and then for years an occasional nugget or a little dust has been found, but NOW the boys, excited by recent discoveries, will flock to the new diggings. The Caribou Mines are nowhere, compared to the new find, and diggings are only twenty or thirty miles from Whatcom – on the South Fork of the Nooksack and Whatcom will soon rival the famous Leadville in its palmiest days.[13]

The editor overstated the case a bit, as he often did, and by the end of 1885 the truth was known – there was no bonanza on the South Fork. Still, men had scoured the area, and the pace of settlement increased.

Settlers gradually established themselves on the North Fork as well. The first one set up housekeeping at Kendall in 1884, at Boulder Creek in 1889, and at Glacier in 1893. Railroads were on everyone's minds in the late 1880s, for they promised great growth and business opportunities, particularly if they were tied to national rail lines. The great aspirations of regional rail promoters were never to materialize, but by 1890 rails were approaching the Mount Baker country from the south, west and north. The days of epic trips to the mountain, when the approach equaled the climb for adventure and difficulty, were rapidly fading. The mountain was opening, and what would be called an "epidemic of mountaineering" was about to begin.

4

The Mountaineering Epidemic

The mountains are fountains not only of rivers and fertile soil, but of men. Therefore we are all, in some sense, mountaineers, and going to the mountains is going home.

— John Muir, 1874

The year 1891 began what Charles Finley Easton, Mount Baker's earliest historian, called the "epidemic of mountaineering." Suddenly people were responding to the sporting challenge of the mountain. The population of the Puget Sound region was growing rapidly. Access to the mountains was improving. Many climbers were ascending Mount Rainier, John Muir among them in 1888. Eloquent writers like Muir were extolling the wonders of mountains and mountain travel for their own sakes. The era of pioneering was coming to a close in the Pacific Northwest, and men and women with a love of outdoor adventure turned to sport instead of frontier exploration.

In late June of 1891 a party of eight local men, six from the town of Blaine and two from Sumas, set out to prospect the lower reaches of the mountain and to climb it if possible. They made their way over dusty, rough roads to Maple Falls, then followed the trail to the mouth of Glacier Creek, where they camped. Above them rose the small but precipitous Church Mountain. No one had climbed this little mountain before, as far as they knew. They accepted the challenge, struggling up steep tree-covered slopes to slide paths of tangled alder, then through alpine meadows to the short rock scramble leading to the summit. The climb was strenuous, but the party was young and strong. They enjoyed the trip immensely. From the top of Church they could look southward and see the summit reaches of Mount Baker gleaming in the sunshine, and they renewed their resolve to climb it.

From their viewpoint the easiest approach to the mountain seemed up Glacier Creek. The milky water of this stream indicated that it flowed from Baker's glaciers. Early summer runoff made the stream roar and leap; they could hear it rolling large bounders beneath its rough surface. They headed upstream, staying as close to it as they could, and found the traveling very difficult. At one point the creek travels through a deep gorge, where they had to negotiate very steep sidehills. They kept at it. After several days of struggle they eventually emerged from the nearly impenetrable brush into a huge basin into which tumbled large glaciers directly off the western and northern sides of the mountain. They had gained little elevation, but they were at last free of the hostile vegetation. Settling down for a rest, they gazed at their gleaming objective far above. Their resting spot was just below the snout of the Roosevelt Glacier at an elevation of approximately four thousand feet. Their only predecessors on this approach had been Coleman, Bennett and Tennant on their attempt in 1866, when they reached the upper slopes of the mountain but could not find their way over a large crevasse onto the summit.

Though it was only noon they were exhausted and decided to camp. Steep gravelly slopes rose north and south of them, and as they reclined they heard a rockslide. Looking up they saw the cause of the slide: several mountain goats were browsing leisurely across the slope above them. The goats had not detected their presence, so two of the men, E.H. Thomas and Richard Smith, grabbed their rifles and set off up the hillside after fresh meat. The going was steep and difficult as the way quickly turned into unstable gravel that made very poor footing. Clouds of dust rose above them as they climbed, and they could not avoid dislodging rocks and boulders, which bounded noisily down the slope. The goats, alerted to danger by all the commotion, started to slip away. The men climbed faster and harder, using their rifles as third legs for stability.

Suddenly Smith's rifle discharged, wounding him in his upper right arm, severing an artery. His heart was pounding hard from the exertion, and blood spurted brightly from the wound. Smith lost consciousness and tumbled headlong down the slope. He fell two hundred feet, sustaining more injuries in the fall. His companions rushed to his aid but could do little for him. His shocked friends buried him on Bastille Ridge and abandoned their aspirations to climb. Thus inauspiciously began the "epidemic of mountaineering."

A thousand feet above this party, several miles to the south, another group was bent on climbing the mountain. Members of this party later claimed they had heard the shot that killed poor Smith. The fact that there were two parties trying to climb at the same time indicates how times were changing in the Mount Baker region. This group of eight men (among them V.V. Lowe, who had accompanied Bales up Sherman Peak five years ear-

An 1892 party on the summit, gathered around the stake (in center) left by the 1891 LaConner party.

lier) had come up the Middle Fork of the Nooksack River. Upon reaching Clearwater Creek, they had followed it to its headwaters, then climbed the divide between Clearwater and Glacier creeks. They were camped high on this divide when they heard the fatal shot.

Unaware of the drama unfolding nearby, they proceeded to make the second complete ascent of the mountain. They went up Grouse Ridge, traversed over to Heliotrope Ridge and made their way onto Coleman Glacier. Traversing beneath the Black Buttes, they gained the saddle between Colfax Peak and the summit, then climbed the Roman Wall to the top. They had little trouble. The weather was warm, the wind light, the view unobstructed, and they were elated. They planted two poles in the snow, unfurled an American flag and struck heroic poses for the first photographs ever taken on the summit. Wandering around, they looked over the sides of the summit plateau, gazed into the crater, and enjoyed their triumph.

Reluctantly and uneventfully, they left the top and descended to their camp, badly sunburned and snowblind. "Smith and Whitetruck," Lowe wrote

Historic Routes to the Summit

Glacier Creek · Skyline Divide · Deadhorse Creek · Cougar Divide · Dobbs Creek · Bar Creek · Ptarmigan Ridge · Camp Kiser · Chowder Ridge · Bastille Ridge · Mazama Glacier · Rainbow Glacier · Rainbow Creek · Kulshan Cabin · Roosevelt Glacier · Park Glacier · Coleman Glacier · Marmot Ridge · Summit · Crater · Boulder Glacier · Park Creek · Black Buttes · Deming Glacier · Sherman Peak · Wallace Creek · Easton Glacier · Middle Fork Nooksack River · Railroad Grade · Sulphur Morraine

Glacier Trail (Marathon Route)
La Conner Party - 1891
1906 Mazama Route
1909 Mazama Route
Deming Trail
(Marathon Route)

afterward, "had their faces in unrecognizable shape and they could not see for some time . . . we were all affected more or less and are not over it yet."[1]

This climb marked the beginning of modern mountaineering on Mount Baker. Some members of the party had come quite a distance to make the climb. Mount Baker's first photographer was W.O. Amsden from Seattle, who was to make another important climb one month later. He made the ninth successful ascent of Mount Rainier, taking some historic photographs along the way.

Photographers had to be dedicated in those days; their equipment was heavy and awkward. Amsden used an eight-by-ten view camera on Mount Baker. A year before Arthur Warner had carried such a photographic outfit to the top of Mount Rainier to take the first photographs there. Warner's camera was eighteen inches long, with a body twelve inches square. The lens had an aperture of $f.22$ and lacked a shutter. Exposures were made by plucking a black cap from the lens and replacing it again. Warner's outfit with its tripod, glass plates and other items, weighed over fifty pounds.[2] Amsden probably used a similar outfit on Mount Baker. Climbing mountains like Rainier and Baker was no easy task in those early days with very long approaches. The photographers who carried such loads and went to such pains to record the early climbs were a truly dedicated and remarkable lot.

The next party to climb Mount Baker in 1891 came at the mountain from an entirely new direction; east, from Baker Lake. The group members – all from LaConner, a small community near the mouth of the Skagit River – were J.O. Boen, "Leader and Photographer"; Sue Nevin and William Land, "Artists"; Charles Beilenberg, "Guide"; Alex Beilenberg, "cook"; S.W. Bailey, "Scribe"; and Robert Woods, "Camp Attendant."[3] Obviously, everyone had his (and her) role on this expedition. In mid-August they traveled by stage from LaConner to the trailhead and followed the trail up Baker River to Baker Lake. The hike up the river was about twenty miles to a smaller lake than is present today; the modern lake is created by a hydroelectric dam. The lake was idyllic, cool and calm in the wilderness solitude of beautiful August days. The party enjoyed the lake so much they spent three days there relaxing and summoning the courage and ambition to take on the strenuous part of the trip. They were camped near the lake at approximately seven hundred feet of elevation and faced a climb of ten thousand feet to the summit. The mountain was only a few miles west of their camp, but a laborious bushwhack would be necessary to reach timberline and the real climbing.

Finally they set out upward. The going was as difficult as they expected. Winding among giant trees, they had to climb under, over, or around huge logs lying on the forest floor. Tangles of devils club, vine maple and other vegetation slowed progress, and they encountered streams and steep climbs as

Sue Nevin, the first woman to climb Mount Baker.

they slowly gained elevation. Fortunately they were in shade much of the time in the two days it took them to reach timberline at the base of Boulder Ridge. They were at an elevation of about four thousand feet, six thousand to go! A day of rest and recovery was necessary before the final push for the summit. The "scribe" recorded their ascent:

> Monday morning the tug of war commenced, and for nine and a half hours we did as hard climbing as any people ever did. We followed as near as possible up the east side of the mountain, part of the time over the brim of a yawning crater where one misstep would have carried us over to death in the abyss below.
>
> As we neared the top we had to get down into crevasses and work our way through them and with the ax cut steps in their opposite sides and climb out again only to find other crevasses ahead of us. We were finally compelled to take to the heights of projecting rocks because of the depth of melting snow and the thick grouping of the crevasses.
>
> When we had thus ascended to within about one hundred feet of the summit we encountered a crevasse in the snow 25 or 30 feet across and 50 or 75 feet deep, the opposite wall of which seemed to be a perpendicular face of ice. Right here we all sat down disheartened and discouraged for it seemed impossible to overcome this final barrier.
>
> Robert Woods, resolving to make one more effort, left the party and found the end of the crevasse where he was enabled to let himself down. After an hour's persistent work with his ax he succeeded in getting up the other side of the crevasse. He was then lost sight of but soon the air was rent with his triumphant whoops, which assured us that he had reached the summit. We followed his steps and, under the inspiration of refreshed courage we were at his side a half-hour later – on the summit, 4:30 o'clock, Monday, August 24.[4]

They had made the first ascent of the Boulder Ridge – Boulder Glacier route, negotiating some tricky crevasses in the section above the ridge. Sue Nevins, the "brave Iowa girl . . . a vivacious young woman just out of her teens" had climbed strongly and, seemingly to the surprise of her male associates, "stood the fatigue of the trip fully as well as did her companions."[5] She was, of course, the first woman to climb the mountain and would be the only woman to climb it until many did so with the Mountaineers party of 1908. The Boen group did not stay on the summit long because it was very cold and

J.M. Edson and P.J. Harris, photographed by E.A. Hegg on their first asent of Twin Sisters, 1891.

late in the day. They faced some tricky down-climbing through the icefall as well. Returning the way they had climbed they reached their timberline camp at 8 p.m. A new and soon-to-be popular route on Mount Baker had been discovered.

Mount Baker was not the only mountain in the region attracting attention in 1891. The Twin Sisters Range, a group of small rocky peaks to the southwest, was visited in August by J.M. Edson, P.J. Harris and E.A. Hegg. This trio made its way to the mountain by way of the Park and Saxon Post Offices to the confluence of Skookum Creek and the South Fork of the Nooksack River. From there they struck eastward for several miles, keeping to the north of the creek. The going was typically rough, untracked, and dense with prickly, clinging vegetation. They finally reached a meadow at the head of a branch of Skookum Creek at the base of the rocky high point of the range, the 6,932-foot South Twin. From there they were able to work their way upward through a narrow gorge, then over boulder fields and talus until they encountered snow and steep rock. The crux of their climb was the summit itself, where "the only foothold is the narrow, irregular shelves and jutting points of rock to be found on an almost perpendicular cliff. This was surmounted with much difficulty and danger, tearing clothing and lacerating fingers . . ."[6] The dunite rock on these crags is unusually abrasive, as all climbers since this first threesome have discovered. Once on the summit they could gaze across a deep cirquie at the North Twin, and beyond that to the great panorama of Mount Baker. A glacier wraps around the South Twin on the east, and many lesser summits of the range stretch off southward. Hoping to learn the elevation of their peak, the trio carried an aneroid barometer on the climb, but all readings were much higher than they knew they should be. Hegg took photographs with his eight-by-ten camera.

The climb was a first. It was also a visit to the heights of the Mount Baker region by a young man who was to distinguish himself later in life with a marvelous photographic record of the Klondike gold rush. E.A. Hegg was twenty-three when he made his South Twin climb. He had been in the Northwest only two years having moved from Wisconsin to Tacoma to seek his fortune as a commercial photographer. The competition in Tacoma was severe, so he moved north to the communities on Bellingham Bay and opened a studio in New Whatcom. Like most commercial photographers he buttered his bread with studio photography, but his first love was outdoor work. He photographed men in nature extensively, recording the activities of fishermen and loggers in the country around New Whatcom. The call of the Klondike captured him in 1897 as it did many of the young men of New Whatcom; he gathered up his ponderous photographic gear and set off. For four years he recorded the drama of the search for gold from Skagway to Nome, compiling a magnificent and unique record of this historic time, most of which has been preserved.[7]

Yet another party came to climb Mount Baker before the close of the 1891 season. This group traveled from Seattle and was led by Major E.S. Ingraham, a Seattle school teacher and mountaineer who already had two successful ascents of Mount Rainier to his credit. With Ingraham were B.K. Coryell, J.V.A. Smith and Fred Calhoun. They came by train to Deming and hiked over rough road and trail to the mouth of Glacier Creek and then Grouse Creek, finally emerging into meadows high on Grouse Ridge. They camped on the ridge and prepared to climb only to be turned back on their first foray by a fierce storm that dumped three feet of new snow on the heights and buckets of rain on the climbers. Finally the weather cleared and they set out again.

> Sunday morning dawned upon us clear and cold, the peaks above us glistening in their mantle of virgin snow. We were awake at four o'clock and ready for the ascent by seven. We followed the same course as on the first attempt, in a general way in an easterly direction. After three hours of hard climbing up the glacier, avoiding numerous crevasses by circuitous routes and crossing others on frail snow bridges, we reached the divide between Colfax and the main peak.
>
> From this point the ascent is very abrupt, the first part of the distance continuing along a ridge covered with volcanic ashes several inches deep. The last 500 feet is a wall of seemingly perpendicular appearance. Ordinarily the mountaineer would have to cut steps up this steep wall of ice, but, on account of the new snow which had fallen, we were enabled to make the ascent by means of our alpenstocks alone.[8]

They reached the summit, enjoyed the spectacular view of mountains all around mantled in new snow, then made their way back to camp. Another storm closed in upon them as they reached their tents; September storms forced the end of high climbing for the year.

The mountain had seemingly let down her guard in 1891. Conditions on and around it had been propitious for climbing. All over the Northwest men and a few women were responding to the challenges of the mountains. Most were rank beginners who could not resist the lure of the dominant features of the landscape looming to the east on clear days. Many were climbers content to "conquer" their local giant, but others like Professor Ingraham were the Northwest's first generation of dedicated mountaineers, people who would climb and explore mountains throughout their lives for no reason other than that they loved to do so.

There is no record of other attempts to climb the mountain until July of 1892, when J.M. Edson, one of the party that made the first ascent of the South Twin the previous summer, prepared for an ascent. Edson's party hoped to establish a new route by approaching the mountain along Skyline Divide and Chowder Ridge, unaware of Dorr's unsuccessful attempt. Instead of traveling up Glacier Creek, Edson's group climbed directly up the forested slopes southeast of the confluence of the creek and the North Fork of the Nooksack River, as Dorr had done in 1884. They emerged into alpine meadows at the top of Skyline Divide and could see that a long ridge walk through open country should take them to a sharp and steep ridge all the way to the summit. They worked their way out along these ridges, enjoying a magnificent view of Baker's north face. Eventually they came to the pinnacle of unconsolidated rock that had thwarted Dorr and named it "Pumice Stone Pinnacle." It proved too much for them, as it had for Dorr. It fell apart under foot and hand. Steep slopes of snow and ice stretched down to dark crevasses on both sides of the rock. There was no hope of going further that way, so they turned back, disappointed.

These men were mountaineers, not prospectors as Dorr and his friends had been, and were not ready to give up their goal. They turned down Bastille

The Morovits cabin.

Ridge from Chowder Ridge, losing 4500 feet of elevation as they dropped all the way down to Glacier Creek. With classic understatement one member of the party wrote later: "We then decided to change our position and the next day moved camp to the head of Glacier Creek, a beautiful place for camping, but much lower down than our former camp."[9] On July 31 the party set out to climb by way of Coleman Glacier, ". . .carrying ropes, axes, and our eatables such as fired grouse, stewed huckleberries, biscuits and cold coffee."[10] Seven hours later they were on the summit and were "good and ready for lunch." The stake left on the summit the previous September by the LaConner party was still there, and they split parts off of it for souvenirs.

> The descent was made by tying ourselves together, turning our faces to the mountain and climbing down backwards for the first thousand feet. The balance of the descent was without any particular incident and we arrived home pretty well worn out though not as badly sunburnt as some of the previous parties.[11]

The summer of 1892 marked the beginning of the career of Mount Baker's first and most unusual mountain guide. His name was Joe Morovits, and he had recently taken up residence in the wilderness meadows at the upper end of Baker Lake. He was building a "ranch" there and prospecting the countryside for gold. Joe was short and stocky, a tough character who became legendary for his feats of strength; over the twenty-seven years that he lived at the foot of Mount Baker's eastern slopes he was called upon many times to assist people who aspired to climb the mountain.

Joe Morovits was born in Wisconsin in 1866 to Bohemian immigrant parents. When he was small, his parents separated and his mother was left to raise seven children. They were poor and life was a struggle. At the age of nine, Joe went to work on a neighbor's farm for a monthly wage of two dollars. He never went to school but learned to read and write from a mining camp bunk-mate when he was twenty-three years old.

As soon as he was able, Joe left home and struck out on his own, working coal mines in Colorado, Idaho, California, on Vancouver Island, and finally in the Blue Canyon Mines at the head of Lake Whatcom, west of Mount Baker. From these mines he moved, at the age of twenty-seven, to the Baker Lake valley – "Morovits country" to a generation of climbers. A letter to Charles Finley Easton describes his life in Baker Lake country:

> I located here two miles west of Baker Lake on the 13th day of October, 1891, built a cabin fit to move into five days later. I lived alone for 27 years. The closest settler was 12 miles down the river.

Mighty Joe Morovits.

There were no trails before me, not even blazes. I wanted to prospect the mountains for precious metals and settled to stay until I could clean up a few hundred thousand dollars. Single-handed I drove over 1000 feet of tunnel and shaft work, have washed down thousands of yards of gravel for placer and have built over 40 miles of trail and kept it open all these years. Other settlers came in after me, but left inside of 6 years, as soon as they proved up on their homesteads and got title to their places. So I have been alone nearly all the time, a Hermit, but a busy one.

I am a jack of all trades. I do iron work and wood work and run my own stamp mill. I put in my own tram, harnessed the water power, took in my own machinery and set it up. I have one piece of iron up there that weighs more than a ton, the mortar.[12]

Joe's feats of strength were legendary – he was the Mount Baker counterpart of the Olympic Mountains' Iron Man of the Hoh. Reportedly Joe thought nothing of carrying a hundred-pound pack the thirty-two miles from the general store in Birdsview to his ranch. That was his standard load, and if he had less weight than that after packing his bacon, flour, beans, ammunition and dynamite, he would make up the difference with whiskey.

He accomplished several truly prodigious feats of strength and ingenuity. Two necessary parts of his mining machinery were a die and shoe for his stamp mill. They weighted 2300 pounds. The mill would allow Joe to crush rocks by dropping the "shoe" onto the die; the ore was crushed in water between the two. After crushing, the rock was washed into a mortar box and the gold taken out. A steamboat delivered the shoe and die to Baker City, the present town of Concrete, and Joe set out to move it over the twenty-one miles to his operation. First he hauled it with four horses, but the trail became too rough for the team after a few miles. So Joe windlassed, or winched, the mortar from tree to tree the rest of the way – it took two years.[13]

Joe appeared on the Mount Baker climbing scene in 1892. In August six LaConner men asked him to lead them up the mountain. Joe had never been up himself but thought he could do it without difficulty. The party made their way past Joe's homestead to Rainbow Creek and up to Rainbow Glacier. They climbed the glacier to the rocky ridge known as Landes Cleaver, from which they could look down to the north into what Joe called the "Hot Springs" – the Dorr Fumaroles. Here four of the party decided they were too exhausted to go further. Joe went on with the other two, up the Cleaver to the "Rocks" – the Cockscomb. Faced here with what seemed insurmountable difficulties, the other two LaConner men gave up. Joe describes what he did:

I was packing my rifle, the Lord only knows why. We were all as green as grass when it came to climb a real mountain. I had lots of experience climbing rough mountains in Colorado, hunting, prospecting and trapping, but never climbed a mountain before that was all covered with snow, and perhaps I wouldn't have gone up Mt. Baker that day, after all the other fellows quit, only we got into an argument. Some said that no man could possibly climb up and I said that any man could go up. So just to prove to the crowd that it could be done, I went and found it a thousand times worse than I figured on. The last rise was near the summit and was the worst. It was so steep that I had to cut notches for every step with the rifle, and, coming down, I had to back down and I had to move around many cracks. The weather was perfect, clear as a bell and warm. We had started at five o'clock in the morning and got back to camp about six in the evening. I went direct on the north side. What I call the hot springs is on the north side at the head of Wells Creek, where there is steam coming out in many places, or fumes.[14]

Thus did Joe begin his climbing career. He made the first solo ascent of Mount Baker along the most difficult route yet climbed on the mountain. It was not repeated until 1906, when a group of skilled and experienced climbers, members of the Portland-based Mazamas, went that way.

Yet another climb counts in this initial "epidemic of mountaineering." In September a group calling itself the "Streetcar Brigade," all employees of the Fairhaven Streetcar Company, successfully climbed the mountain from the Baker Lake side, though little is known of their exact route.

All of this activity – six parties to the summit in two years – indicates that Mount Baker had become a favorite objective of Northwest adventurers. Access to the area had improved, and people had the leisure and inclination to venture onto the mountain for sport. Successful climbs reported by the press lured other aspirants to the mountain's glaciers. A climb to the summit had become almost commonplace.

5

Gold Mines and Foresters

Wise forest production does not mean the withdrawal of forest resources, whether of wood, water, or grass, from contributing their full share to the welfare of the people, but, on the contrary, gives the assurance of larger and more certain supplies. The fundamental idea of forestry is the perpetuation of forests by use. Forest production is not an end of itself; it is a means to increase and sustain the resources of our country and the industries which depend upon them.

— President Theodore Roosevelt
State of the Union Message, 1901

After the first period of mountaineering in the early 1890s, the pace of climbing on Mount Baker slowed considerably for various reasons. The novelty of climbing the mountain was gone. So many people had been to the summit that it was not the unusual achievement it had been in the early '90s. Further, the economic fortunes of the region, indeed of the entire United States, were at an ebb. Bust followed boom. Banks failed and many people were without work. The depression dragged on from 1892 to 1898. Men struggling to survive were not interested in climbing for sport. And increased interest in gold in the Mount Baker region and elsewhere diminished the effort devoted merely to climbing. The mid and late '90s saw gold rushes up the North Fork of the Nooksack and, on a far greater scale, to the Klondike. The adventurous rushed off to make their fortunes and were gone for years in which they often had their fill of hardship. Whatever the reason, fewer people ventured onto the slopes of Mount Baker in the late 1890s and early 1900s.

The idea for a road across the North Cascades was still alive in 1894, when the road commissioners hired a pair of reputable surveyors to make one last cruise through the Mount Baker country to search for a feasible route. Bert Huntoon and H.M. Wellman were hired for the job. They went up the

Bert Huntoon, a figure in the history of the region for forty years.

South Fork of the Nooksack to its headwaters and after several strenuous days they found themselves at "Baker Pass" immediately south of the mountain. Huntoon decided it was time for "a day off," so he and Wellman made a side trip up the glaciers on Baker's south slopes. His terse journal reported:

> At 8 o'clock A.M., we began the ascent of Mt. Baker to obtain what information we could regarding the physical characteristics of the country to be cruised. Our route led us over the big south glacier and winding our way around immense crevasses, we reached the crater at 12:20 p.m., after which it took us 1½ hours to climb to the summit one-fourth mile farther.[1]

That was all there was to it for Huntoon – the climb was no big deal. After the climb they went down to Baker River, up Swift Creek to Austin Pass, then out via the North Fork of the Nooksack. They "circumnavigated" the mountain, quite a feat in itself, and returned to New Whatcom with the opinion that no good route for the proposed road existed, which killed any idea of building across the mountains from the headwaters of the Nooksack River.

While Huntoon and Wellman were walking around Mount Baker, a group of climbers was gathering on the slopes of Mount Hood to form a new climbing club called the Mazamas. They were very enthusiastic about climbing throughout the Northwest, and during the summer of 1895 set out on an ambitious plan to heliograph, or flash messages with mirrors, from Mount Baker in the north to Mount Shasta in the south. Mazamas, all carrying heliography equipment, would climb Mounts Baker, Rainier, St. Helens, Adams, Hood, Jefferson, Diamond Peak, Three Sisters, Pitt and Shasta on the 9th of July. Weather permitting, they would relay flash messages the entire length of the Cascade Range.

The Mount Baker party, each man with his Merriam pack filled with clothing, appropriate equipment and two double blankets rolled, traveled by train from Portland to Seattle where they caught the steamer *State of Washington* north to New Whatcom. From there they took another train to Sumas, where their packer, William Thompson, was awaiting them with three horses. In addition to their personal gear and food they had "a copper box for records which we expected to leave on the mountain, barometers, cameras, and four carrier pigeons."[2] They set off immediately for the mountain, staying the first night at one of Thompson's cabins, twelve miles along the way, and the second night at his last cabin, fifteen miles further, beyond Glacier Creek on Thompson Creek.

The men could look up Glacier Creek and see their goal at its head. An argument rose over how they should approach the mountain. Why not go up

Glacier Creek, they suggested. But the packer assured them that the shortest and best route to the mountain was up the ridge rising immediately behind his cabin. He claimed to have almost reached the summit by that route, and "practically refused to go the way we had chosen." Thompson prevailed, and the next morning the men found themselves struggling through blowdowns on a steep hillside. One Mazama observed:

> Other parties had gone up Glacier Creek canyon which we were leaving to our right. We were strongly advised by the men who had made the trial that way, and by Thompson, that the fatigues and perils being fearful and the possibilities of perishing being considerable, to avoid it. But our way by this time was proving anything but comfortable.[54]

They climbed high on the ridge, cached their food and equipment and went back down to ferry a second load up the next morning. As they descended they were overtaken by darkness and became lost. They had a bad time "passing through ill-smelling damp thickets of devils-clubs" until, with the aid of a full moon, they finally reached Glacier Creek and followed it down to Thompson's cabin. Their expedition had not started well.

The next day they headed back up through the steep brush, reached their cache and proceeded on, eventually climbing out of the woods and into the subalpine parkland on the top of Skyline Divide. They worked their way out along the ridge system only to realize, as had Dorr several years earlier, that they could not reach the summit. Their "guide" had led them astray. "It was now very late in the afternoon. We were stuck up against the very sky at the extreme limit of vegetation, higher than any of the other points around us, with the great, deep canyon of Glacier Creek between us and the opposite side, the way that now looked feasible and the one we first planned on taking."

It seemed unlikely that they would make their heliography appointment, which was scheduled for the next day, but they were determined to be the first Mazamas to climb the mountain. They would have to drop down two thousand feet to Glacier Creek and make their way to the summit over Coleman Glacier. Descending Bastille Ridge, they encountered further trouble. One fellow "was carrying a 36-inch mercurial barometer strapped to his pack, when in some way it caught and tripped him, falling among some rocks and knotty logs, injuring him internally." They found a fairly level spot on the steep hillside and pitched camp.

All aspiration to climb the mountain was abandoned. For two days they perched there on the steep side of Bastille Ridge while the injured man recovered enough to travel. They scouted a way out while they waited. Smith Creek drained the west slope of the ridge and offered the easiest descent. So with their supplies completely exhausted, they descended this creek to where it met Glacier Creek just above its gorge. They camped here and "were fortunate to kill a mess of fish with boulders." They then struggled down Glacier Creek, climbing up and down, traversing sidehills, hanging on to shrubbery and devil's club and fighting their way through alder thickets. Much the worse for wear, they eventually reached their guide's cabin at Thompson Creek and ate several huge meals while barely restraining their desire to wreak revenge on the incompetent guide who had gotten them into trouble. After a night's rest, they hiked the twenty-seven miles to Sumas in eight hours, finding the trail delightful after the horrible conditions they had struggled through on previous days.

The heliograph plan was obviously a failure, and the ill-fated party had no opportunity to use any of the equipment they lugged so laboriously over the countryside. The copper box they were going to leave on the summit went back to Portland with them. The carrier pigeons purchased in Seattle were sent from the mountain with messages but were never heard from. In a letter to Charles Finley Easton in 1912, Martin W. Gorman of the Mazamas added a humorous postscript to his account of the trip. They had such a hard time of it that upon reaching Sumas on the return trip, "one man's clothing was so badly torn that he had to be left out in the woods until the others borrowed some extra garments from the hotel keeper to fix him up for the occasion." A tired, sore and frustrated group of Mazamas boarded the train in Sumas for the trip home. Despite this disappointment the Mazamas would soon return and make their mark on the mountain.

William Thompson was never again asked to serve as guide for the Mazamas, but his failure with them did little to hurt his packing business up the North Fork. While the Mazamas were on the mountain, and for several years thereafter, exploration for gold in the Mount Baker region was increasing. Various "strikes" gave Thompson and other packers all they could do to serve the hundreds, sometimes thousands, of gold-seekers who streamed up the Nooksack valley. Hamilton Wells and Charles Bagley, two local men whose names are now attached to creeks north of the mountain, predicted after a prospecting trip far up the North Fork in 1891 that gold would most surely be found somewhere in the upper Nooksack country. Time would prove them correct.

Access to the region was improving. The aborted scheme to cross the mountains with a road resulted in an improved road and trail up the river. By the end of 1893 a rough wagon road extended as far as Boulder Creek, a few miles below Glacier. Beyond that the "Cascade State Trail" was improved all the way to Ruth Creek, near the headwaters of the North Fork. Horses could be used on this trail. Scattered settlers were moving into the upper North Fork valley: A.B. Loop to Boulder Creek in 1889, C.C. Cornell and William Thompson to Glacier in 1893.

Many panned and dug for gold in the region. Several found it, most notably Hamilton Wells, Jack Post, Russ Lambert and Lyman G. Valkenberg. Wells, a Union Army drummer boy during the Civil War, settled in New Whatcom in 1887. An avid outdoorsman, he hunted, explored, and prospected up the North Fork whenever he could get away. In the early 1890s he found color in Ruth Creek and was convinced that a lode was to be found nearby. His certainly and enthusiasm drew other men into the Ruth Creek area. In 1896 he located what he called the "Silver Tip" lode on Ruth Creek, touching off a flurry of activity in that area. Wells never made any money, but he kept the dream alive crawling all over the hills and mountains north of Mount Baker.

Jack Post was an old-timer by the time Wells came on the scene. He had come from somewhere during the Fraser River Gold Rush of 1858. For forty years, on and off, he poked around the hills looking for gold, operating out of the thriving little community of Sumas, on the International Boundary just west of the mountain foothills. All those years he found little until, in the mid-1890s, he and two Sumas friends made the biggest strike in the history of the Mount Baker region.

Russ Lambert, the "White Collar Prospector," was in on this strike. He was a Sumas attorney who met Jack Post in town shortly after hanging his lawyer's shingle there in 1889. Lyman G. Valkenberg was the other of Post's Sumas partners, a logger and homesteader who had lived in the Nooksack Valley since 1882. Post had found gold in Swamp Creek, which flowed from the north into the Nooksack about a mile downstream from its confluence with Ruth Creek. He traced Swamp Creek to its source near Twin Lakes, nestled at five thousand feet between two small mountains. Tracings of gold were also unearthed around the lakes. Most significant were boulders of rich quartz in the bed of Silesia Creek, which flowed northeastward just north of the lakes. Post was getting along in years and knew that considerable exploring would be necessary to discover the source of the gold and quartz, so he enlisted the relatively inexperienced Lambert and Valkenberg to assist him. They needed little urging.

The three men had promising claims on Ruth Creek, but these claims assayed toward copper and silver, much less valuable than gold. The three were working their Ruth Creek claims in August, 1897 when they decided it was time to look for more promising prospects around Twin Lakes. On August 22, they camped by Twin Lakes, at the foot of Winchester Mountain,

Packing into the Lone Jack Mine, 1920s.

in Skagway Pass. Dividing up the ground to be covered, they were off with high hopes at dawn on the 23rd.

Valkenberg and Lambert found nothing and were stirring their beanpot in camp by the lakes late in the evening when Post came shouting into camp. He had found what he was seeking – a thick quartz outcropping extending across the face of Bear Mountain just north of the lakes which was "fairly bristling" with flecks of gold "as large as peas."[4] Post was sure they had something big, the "mother lode" for which he had been searching for forty years, the dream that keeps every prospector going. We can imagine the three men whooping and hollering and dancing around their fire. Their speculation must have been rampant; undoubtedly a few toasts, if only of coffee, must have been drunk to their prospects. For two days the three set their stakes, marked their claims, and gathered ore samples. Then Lambert set out down Swamp Creek and the Nooksack River to Sumas for supplies and assays.

The men named their find Lone Jack. When Lambert got the assay report he was flabbergasted – "Gold value of ore assayed $10,750 per ton."[5] He had to go to New Whatcom to record the claims, and word spread like wildfire through the community that something big was happening up the river. The assay report struck Sumas like a bolt of lightning – business ground to a halt in the excitement. Lambert secured supplies, packed his ponies, and headed out again for Twin Lakes. Many others were not far behind. The greatest gold rush in the history of the Mount Baker region was on. Local historian Percival Jeffcott describes what happened:

> The three prospectors at once continued their extensive explorations on their five claims in the Post-Lambert Group, but scarcely had they gotten well started, when the first of the vanguard of the now increasing Gold Rush began appearing in the little pocket in the mountains around Twin Lakes, and, pitching their tents, started an intensive search of the vicinity of the big strike for good locations. Almost overnight, the camp mushroomed to near the size of a village; and, visioning the growth of a permanent mining camp, they called it "Union City." Within the course of several weeks, there were 300 to 500 men in the "City" of tents, and before snow fell, as many as 300 claims had been staked in the Lone Jack vicinity. But hundreds of other prospectors were arriving, and fanning out in other parts of the North Fork District, established camps at the mouth of Swamp Creek, called "Trail City"; at the mouth of Ruth Creek, called "Wilson's Townsite"; at the 18 Mile Post on Ruth Creek, known as "Gold City"; and at the present site of Shuksan, which took the name of "Gold Hill", because of its proximity to the big strike on Bear Mountain.[6]

Towns appeared literally overnight at these spots in the upper Nooksack valley. The town of Sumas, home of the three fortunate prospectors who started the rush, was virtually emptied of men within hours of Lambert's departure. One fellow there was reportedly moving his house when he heard the news of the strike. Leaving the house in the middle of the street, he threw together an outfit and headed for the prospects. The paper in New Whatcom reported:

> All hours of the day, may be seen on the streets of the City men starting out in wagons, on horseback, on bicycles and on foot with picks, guns, blankets and provisions, carried in many different ways. Guns, packsaddles, horses, mining location notices, were all in great demand. . . . Everyone seems to be going.[7]

Thousands of feet, horse and human, churned the trail up the Nooksack into a quagmire, and men swarmed over the hills until the snow drove them out in October.

In 1898 they flocked back upriver as soon as snow allowed. Thirty cabins

The Lone Jack Mine near Twin Lakes in 1923, shortly before the end of its period of greatest productivity.

were built at Shuksan just west of where Swamp Creek enters the Nooksack. Two stores and a post office also opened. Post, Lambert and Valkenberg sold their mine to a Portland syndicate; this company proceeded rapidly with development. Bridges were built across the Nooksack in several places, and the road was improved so that mining machinery could be taken to the area. The Lone Jack was sold again in 1899, and by 1902 the mine, the aerial tram for transporting ore, and the stamp mill for processing it were all operating. The mining industry had finally and truly come to the Mount Baker region. The Lone Jack plant burned down, was rebuilt, and was destroyed by avalanches in years to come, but before it was played out more than a million dollars' worth of gold was taken from the mine.

The Gargett Brothers transporting supplies to their mine early in the twentieth century.

Other gold-bearing locations were found. A rich outcropping of gold-bearing quartz was discovered in 1899 about a half mile above the mouth of Wells Creek. A one-mile spur road was extended to it from the State Trail, and the Excelsior Mine eventually went into operation. Never profitable, Excelsior shut down in 1916. A prospector named Tom Braithwaite, so the story goes, was out hunting goats when he discovered what proved to be the second richest vein in the region. He and a companion were on Red Mountain, now Mount Larrabee, on their hunt, and made a long-range shot at a goat. The wounded goat tumbled down the mountainside, and when the hunters reached it they were astounded to see a ledge of quartz flecked with gold. This proved to be the Boundary Red Mountain Gold Mine ledge, just south of the International Boundary. It was to yield some one and half million dollars worth of gold.

Prospectors have been combing the hills in number around Mount Baker ever since the 1898 Gold Rush. Other finds have been made, but none have paid much. Over five thousand mining claims have been filed in the district, but only the Lone Jack and Boundary Red have yielded profit. Of course, all this activity played a large part in the gradual opening of the region. Roads and bridges were built; thousands of people came in contact with the mountain, if only visually. The way was made easier for the large groups of mountaineers who would come to climb the mountain in the next decade.

Credit should be give to these prospectors for their climbing feats. For them, climbing was only a means to an end, but when we follow their foot-steps today through the mountains between Baker and the International Boundary, we marvel at the rough and exposed places they traveled. They were not out for sport so never recorded their climbing exploits. But the cheechacos and sourdoughs, driven by visions of riches and glory, risked their lives countless times in places where modern climbers break out the rope. The story of prospectors' climbing in the region cannot be told, but it must be acknowledged.

After he and his partners sold the Lone Jack, Jack Post continued his love affair with the Mount Baker region, this time as one of its first "forest guards." Post could thank the newly born conservation movement for his job. Increasing public concern over exploitation of the public domain had led Congress in 1891 to give the president power to establish forest reserves. They would be administered by the General Land Office under the jurisdiction of the Department of the Interior. Before his term expired, President Benjamin Harrison set aside thirteen million acres of such reserves. No means of administering the forests were established; they were simply closed to private exploitation. In 1897, President Grover Cleveland proclaimed another twenty million acres reserved, among them the Washington Forest Reserve, which included the Mount Baker region.

At the outset the status of "reserve" did not provide much protection. No management plans were formulated and no funds were available to hire anyone to protect the resources. That began to change around 1900 and Jack Post was one of the first to be hired as a General Land Office forest guard. The equipment and instructions he received illustrate the kind of resources he had to work with and the vagueness of his charge. He was given a small axe, a rake, a brushhook, a pitchfork, and the following instructions: "take care of the forest, rake up leaves, clean up debris, build cabins, etc., for superior officers."[8]

When western politician's initial outrage at this "land grab" subsided (western congressmen were, then as now, often strongly pro-development), Congress acted to define purpose and set up management for the reserves. The forests were to be protected from destruction, but timber was to be sold in a controlled way. A principle of use and a system of supervision and admin-istration were established under the Department of the Interior. The program was, however, one of custody rather than real management and use.

In 1898 a young forester named Gifford Pinchot became Chief of the Division of Forestry in the Department of Agriculture. While his group had no control over the forest reserves, he developed an effective organization within his limited jurisdiction and worked to transfer the reserves from the Department of the Interior to the Department of Agriculture. He achieved

Visitors at the Boundary Red Mountain Mine.

this goal in 1905. President Theodore Roosevelt, who supported Pinchot's ideas, pushed the Transfer Act of 1905 through Congress. Pinchot's division became the United States Forest Service, and a new character appeared on the scene – the forest ranger.

The earliest rangers in the Mount Baker region were not trained foresters like Pinchot, but local men who knew the country and possessed the skills needed to establish a lawful presence on the land. Jack Post was one such man. John W. Barber, who was appointed to the North Fork Nooksack District of the Washington Forest Reserve in 1899, was another. A brief article about him appeared in the New Whatcom paper at the time.

> Barber is an old pioneer in the mountains and is familiar with the area to which he has been assigned, having lived there since 1893. He has worked as a woodsman, pioneer, hunter and trapper and is known all over as Daniel Boone of Blaine.
>
> Barber will build cabins at Glacier Creek and at the twenty milepost on the Cascade State Road, at both of which places he expects to keep a headquarters. He is very much alive to the necessity of keeping fires out of our National Forests.[9]

Early rangers like Post, Barber, O.G. Armstrong, Carl Bell, and Joe Ridley had to be jacks-of-all-trades, able to work with axe, saw, hammer, transit, pack animal, mason's trowel, and various mechanical gadgets. Qualifying for the job of ranger was not easy, as C.C. McGuire notes in his memoirs.

> As memory serves me, the following tests were given: (1) From the foliage, identify ten species of trees grown on the Mt. Baker – give common and technical names – if you can spell the latter, more power to you. (2) Fall a tree ten or more inches in diameter with an axe. In giving this test a stake was driven in the ground about twenty feet from the tree. The victim was allowed to select the point where the stake was driven. All he had to do then was to fall the tree so that it would drive the stake further into the ground. His skill was determined by the nearness of the tree bole to the stake. Only three candidates out of sixteen survived that test, one man actually driving the stake. Most trees went wide of the mark with some trees falling in the opposite direction. (3) Figure magnetic declinations on the four quadrants of the compass. . . . (4) Run and pace a triangle; prepare the field notes and compute the acreage. (5) Demonstrate your ability to use a seven-foot crosscut saw. (6) Tell the boss what ingredients and how much each you

would use in preparing a batch of biscuits. (7) Build and put out a campfire. . . . (8) Pack a horse. This was a toughy. . . . Not only was your skill tested but you worked against time. Many would-be rangers fell by the wayside on this test. One bewildered candidate got the pack saddle on backwards with the britchen over the horse's head and used the breast strap for a double hitch.[10]

Men who passed the test worked on patrolling their territory, building trails, bridges and cabins. The first Forest Service headquarters in the Mount Baker region was built on Gallop Creek, in the town of Glacier, in 1907. A four-room dwelling with no plumbing or other conveniences, a shop, warehouse and barn made up the station. Rangers Joe Ridley and Carl Bell built the Deming Ranger Station in 1908 at the National Forest Boundary. Bell lived there with his wife and three sons, keeping the station open for hikers once a trail was built up the river in 1909.

Life was often tough for these early rangers, but that was one reason they signed on. They enjoyed the challenges of travel in rugged country, of exploring and protecting their vast domain. In 1908 the Washington Forest Reserve was divided up into four "national forests": the Chelan, Wenatchee, Snoqualmie, and Washington National Forests. The latter, which included the Mount Baker region (the name was changed to Mount Baker National Forest in 1926), in turn was divided into four districts. Parts of the Mount Baker region fell into the North Fork Nooksack District No. 1 (later the Glacier Ranger District) and the Baker River District No. 2. These were big areas, the North Fork District encompassing 225,860 acres.

Patrolling such territories for fire and various illegal activities often took rangers into the field for weeks or even months. They often transferred between districts as work required more men here or there. McGuire spent three years bounding around the Baker River and Nooksack districts; his feelings about finally becoming a "district" ranger at Glacier in 1913 tell much about the life these men led.

> I had a wife and two children and began to wonder if in this job of Forest Ranger I would ever get to live with them, but that spring Ranger Jones quit and I got the Glacier Station. Here, for the first time, I felt that I definitely had a job, could have my family with me and need not wonder where I would land next. The Ranger's house was a four-room affair, each room ten by twelve, no plumbing or built-in "folderols." A fireplace was built in the center of the building but at its best it made a good smoke house, and at its worst, well, we just moved outside until the fire went out. My

Early logger.

first Sunday I started tearing it out. . . . I laid up the brick for the chimney and my wife carried the hod. We lived in this shack for 6 years. The house also served as an office and the dining room table was my desk . . . .[11]

The United States Forest Service would from this time manage and administer the Mount Baker region. They attempted to mediate conflicting demands for use of the area's resources and determined in large measure how men and women would change the environment of the mountain and its surroundings.

There was still more federal government involvement in the area. By executive order of May 10, 1899, Baker Lake and surrounding lands within one-half mile of the shore were reserved for the use of the United States Commissioner of Fish and Fisheries for a "fish cultural station." Construction of a hatchery was begun, and a salmon production program started in 1907. This installation included improvement of the trail and ultimately the construction of a road into the Baker Lake area. An ill-fated facility, its operation was interrupted three times, twice by fire and once by a crushing snowpack. The hatchery operated until 1940, when the land and improvements were transferred from the Bureau of Fisheries to the Forest Service.

A few people were climbing Mount Baker while the politicians and bureaucrats were deciding how the area should be managed and the forest rangers were making their first tentative efforts. Joe Morovits, untouched by activities in Washington, D.C. and the gold rushes to the North Fork and the Klondike (he certainly knew of the latter, for his brother, who homesteaded near him for two years, headed north with the Argonauts in 1897), continued his prospecting and climbing. He climbed Boulder Ridge in July 1894, and traveled the same route again in each of the next two summers. His brother, newly arrived in 1895, joined him for the climb that year. He made his fifth ascent in 1900, leading a party of eight up Boulder Ridge. Their climb was uneventful but significant because it introduced John A. Lee to the mountain. Lee, the principal of New Whatcom High School, would soon move to Portland to practice law. He would become a member and leader of the Mazamas, and would return to Mount Baker many times. Also in the party were a forest ranger and two instructors from the State Normal School, a college which would pour a stream of eager young climbers onto the mountain for various adventures and misadventures in years to come.[12]

The mountain was climbed again in 1903 by one of the most experienced Northwest climbers of the day – C.E. Rusk. Rusk came to the mountain twice, succeeding on his second try. His wife was with him the first time. They made a long hike from Baker City to timberline on Boulder Ridge, only to be frustrated there by a storm. On his second attempt a few weeks later he was joined by George Cantwell, a photographer, and W.A. Alexander. They ascended Boulder Ridge, Cantwell and Rusk finding a new way to finish the climb. Instead of angling leftward from the top of the ridge and finishing the climb on Boulder Glacier, they went up slightly to the right. This required delicate negotiation of unstable rock just below the summit of Grant Peak. The rock took a long time to climb. They were late arriving on the summit and were benighted on Boulder Ridge. According to Rusk's account, they descended in the dark without incident and thoroughly enjoyed the climb.[13]

6

Mountaineering Clubs
Open Mount Baker

A trip into the Mount Baker country every season for a couple of weeks or more, will most assuredly improve the health in every way. Besides, your disposition will be greatly improved, and that grouch you had against everyone you met, will disappear into thin air, just like the clouds disappear from the dome of Mount Baker in the early morning at sunrise. Take a "hike" up on the eastern slopes of the mountain some morning and view the glorious sunrise, and you will feel better toward all mankind ever afterwards.
— L.R. Markley, M.D., 1913

A group of people came together in Oregon in 1884 and formed the Pacific Northwest's first mountaineering group, the Oregon Alpine Club. The idea for the club was undoubtedly inspired by the Appalachian Mountain Club, the first such American club, founded in 1876. The world's first Alpine Club had been formed in 1857 by a group of Englishmen who were enthusiastically developing the sport of mountaineering (often rationalized as contributing to science) in the European Alps. Following the English lead, many such clubs had formed throughout Europe in the 1860s and 1870s and the idea took hold in America.

These clubs often gathered to socialize as well as hike and climb, and before many years passed, an element in the Oregon Alpine Club began to grumble about the direction the club was taking. There were, they thought, too many "elevator riding mountaineers" bent on submerging the original character of the club.[1] So, in 1894, the "true mountaineers" of the Oregon Alpine Club formed a new group, which would be "Composed exclusively of *real* mountain climbers."[2] To make sure that only serious mountaineers would found the group, "this club was to be voted into being upon the icy summit

"THE CORNICE" — BRIM OF THE FLAT-TOPPED SUMMIT

Mountaineers probing for a crevasse, 1908.

of majestic Mount Hood."[3] This was accomplished, a Chinook Indian motto "Nesika Klatawa Sahale" or "We Climb High!" was adopted, and the group took the name Mazamas, or "mountain goats." This was the group that had made the ill-fated heliograph expedition to the mountain described earlier.

The Mazamas instituted a program of annual outings, beginning with the trip to Crater Lake in 1896. These were large undertakings. Many people went, some to climb, some not, but all to enjoy the mountains. After the Crater Lake trip the group established a habit of visiting the Northwest's large volcanoes – Mounts Rainier, Adams, Jefferson, Hood, Adams, the Three Sisters and Shasta in the next decade. They chose Mount Baker as the object of their 1906 annual outing.

Preparations began well in advance of the trip; the group would be a large one requiring a considerable string of pack horses to carry their equipment and food to base camp. They intended to go to the north side of the mountain, which had not been explored extensively. To do this a trail for their pack train must be built. Correspondence flew back and forth between club officers and the Washington Forest Reserve office in Sumas. The Forest Service eventually agreed to construct a trail to a point where the climbers could reach the northern and eastern slopes of the mountain. Rangers needed a trail into the area anyway because they were seeking a route from Nooksack River valley to the Baker River valley. They had been taking a long route around the foothills to the west of Mount Baker and the Twin Sisters. A trail had already been built up the Baker River valley and Swift Creek for several miles, and the foresters thought they could connect the new trail with this one thus helping the rangers cover their large territories.

During the last week of July no less than 118 Mazamas gathered at Sumas. Packers and horses were waiting for them with their supplies. The size of the task of transporting this group is revealed by the number of eggs packed and ready to go – two hundred dozen! The caravan set off up the road to Glacier and beyond to where the new trail left the river and climbed south toward Mount Baker. The trail went up Wells Creek then over the northern shoulder of Slate Mountain and down to a group of subalpine lakes nestled below the western cliffs of Table Mountain. Their base camp, named Camp Sholes in honor of the club president, was pitched at the edge of Hayes Lake. The lakes were collectively known as Galena Lakes to the prospectors who had poked into the hills around them. The Mazamas named them Chain Lakes and ultimately the compromise name of Galena Chain Lakes became their official designation.

Three scouting parties went out to locate a route to Mount Baker's summit. A ridge, which the group named Ptarmigan Ridge, extends from Table Mountain four miles to the northeast base of Baker where scouting parties could step onto the glaciers that gradually rise to the summit. One party turned southeastward onto Park Glacier but could not go far because of crevasses. The other climbed high on the peak, eventually reaching Pumice Stone Pinnacle. They could not get around this obstruction but thought that with more people and time they might be able to find a way over or around it. Scouts returned to Camp Sholes confident that, with the skilled leadership of people like Asahel Curtis and other veterans of Mounts Hood, Adams and Rainier, a way up would certainly be found.

While the scouting parties were out, the rest of the group enjoyed themselves at Camp Sholes. A high cliff loomed above their tents, forming the western edge of Table Mountain. The group made various short but exciting climbs on this cliff, which they called Mazama Dome. They went swimming in the third lake in the chain, which they called Natatorium Lake – the women swam in the forenoon, the men in the afternoon. Most were city dwellers, and they marveled at the perseverance of a pair of gold miners, Arbuthnot and Davis, who had tunneled through a big rocky ridge in the

LAST CLIMB

Mazama hotshots scaled the summit while their companions slept in camp below,
1906.

1890s and lowered the fourth lake nine feet to reach a vein of ore. The weather was good, though mosquitoes were abundant, and they all took their meals together around a large table built by their enterprising cooks.

On August 4, pack horses were loaded and thirty-five climbers set out to climb the mountain. Hiking out Ptarmigan Ridge, they passed a sharp pinnacle which they named Coleman Peak in honor of Edmund T. Coleman. They needed fuel for cooking fires, so made camp near the last available firewood and named the place Camp Kiser, in honor of the outing's leader, F.H. Kiser of Portland.

Early next morning, in clear weather, the party roped up and set off on their climb. They figured they had about four and half miles to travel to the top, which seemed reasonable. Crossing Rainbow Glacier they found the traveling very slow because of extensive crevasses. Passing these, they climbed a ridge of rotten rock. To their right was another glacial expanse, which they named in honor of their organization.

One member of the party, Henry Landes, was the Washington State Geologist and a geology professor at the University of Washington. Looking down onto Mazama Glacier he spotted the Dorr Fumeroles and, with his brother, gave up the climb and descended to explore them. They found an area completely surrounded by glacier, some two acres in extent and actively steaming. Hot springs abounded, forming steaming streams that ran under the ice. The air was acrid with sulphur.

The other thirty-three continued upward, reaching Pumice Stone Pinnacle at three o'clock. They probably did not know that other parties had visited this spot, though coming from another direction, and been stopped by the formation. As pioneering mountaineers they would not have been discouraged by the earlier defeats anyhow, since they were accustomed to overcoming obstacles judged unclimbable by earlier generations. While most of the group tiredly sat on what they called the "Hill of Patience," looking beyond the rotten pinnacle to the summit so tantalizingly close, nine of the best climbers sought a way around the obstacle. Huge crevasses blocked them, but they thought they could surpass them with time. The hour, though, was late and when, after fives hours of work, they had not overcome the problems, they gave up the attempt, and the whole frustrated party returned to Camp Kiser.

Next morning, before most of the party was awake, Kiser and five others walked quietly out of camp. Only the strongest climbers were included, and they left before others who might wish to go were awake – a ploy that led to bitter feelings later. Retracing their track of the previous day they were soon at work on a route around the pinnacle. The party included Kiser, Curtis, Lee (who had climbed the mountain six years earlier with Morovits), Rodney Glisan and two others. These six traversed below the pinnacle, eventually

Major Pioneering Club Outings

Map legend:
- ——————— 1906 Mazamas
- .... 1908 Mountaineers
- —·—·—·—·— 1909 Mazamas

Locations labeled on the map include: American Border Pk, Mt Larrabee, Boundary Red Mine, Tomyhoi Peak, Church Mtn, Twin Lakes, Lone Jack Mine, Goat Mtn, Silesia Creek, Swamp Creek, Canyon Creek, Ruth Creek, Grandy Mtn, North Fork Nooksack River, Excelsior Mine, Mt Sefrit, Hannegan Pass, Chilliwack River, GLACIER, White Creek, Mt Herman, Ski Area, Ruth Mtn, Icy Peak, Glacier Creek, Table Mtn, Mt Shuksan, Razorhorse Creek, Hadley Peak, Coleman Pinnacle, Baker River, Grouse Butte, Coleman Glacier, Mt Baker, Eagle Creek, Shuksan Creek, Easton Glacier, Morovits Ranch, Middle Fork Nooksack River, Boulder Creek, Baker Lake, Sandy Pass, Loomis Mtn, Sulphur Creek, Koma Kulshan Ranger Station, Dock Butte, Twin Sisters Mtn, South Fork Nooksack River, Goat Mtn, Baker River, Dibsud Buttes, Dibsud Creek, CONCRETE, Jackman Creek, Skagit River

99

"THE SIX IMMORTALS", SUCCESS OF 1906.

"The six immortals" on successful climb of upper Park Glacier. Asahel Curtis, the sixth "immortal," is behind the camera.

surmounting steep slopes and the bergshrund and climbed onto the summit plateau. To their surprise, they found a copy of the Mazama prospectus on the summit, left there the previous day, August 6, by C.C. Cornell, an early resident of Glacier, and a Mr. Stewart of Blaine. These two had traversed across Park Glacier while the large Mazama group was climbing toward the pinnacle. They had stayed high, avoiding the crevasses lower on the glacier and had finished the climb from Boulder Ridge.

Kiser and his group were elated nonetheless, for they thought they had pioneered a new route on the mountain. They had indeed made a difficult climb, but the amazing and fearless Joe Morovits had preceded them by fourteen years, hacking steps with his rifle butt. A Mazama summit register was placed on the highest point and the group returned to Camp Sholes.

Curtis, Lee and Glisan had climbed the big one but were ready for more. As Curtis traveled back and forth along Ptarmigan Ridge, he eyed Mount Shuksan's bulky form towering to the east. The climb looked difficult. Hung with glaciers, its summit a sharp spire, Shuksan's western walls looked steep and forbidding. As far as Curtis knew, no one had yet reached the summit, so he decided to try for the first ascent.

Curtis was thirty-two years old. In 1887 he and his brother Edward had moved with their family to Seattle. When their father died in the early 1890s, both young men became professional photographers. Edward specialized in photographic studies of Native Americans, which were to make him famous; Asahel embarked on a career as a commercial photographer. He was already known for his excellent mountain photography and would go on to pioneer the use of photography as a tool for the promotion of economic development of the State of Washington and the City of Seattle. For the moment, however, he was focused on another goal – Mount Shuksan.

Joined by another eager young climber, Montelius Price, Curtis set off from Camp Sholes. The two crossed the broad summit of Table Mountain, then walked across Austin Pass and along the ridge known as Shuksan Arm. When viewed from Table Mountain, this seemed a feasible approach, for it looked like the ridge joined the main body of Shuksan just west of the summit. But the ridge proved very difficult traveling, and the climbers were forced into a deep gorge west of the mountain's southwest wall. Curtis and Price persisted, but after fourteen hours found themselves, late in the day, looking from a crag "almost directly beneath the main summit, but separated from it by great glaciers deep with crevasses. A way might be found through this maze, but it would require days of work."[4] They gave up the attempt and made the long trip back to camp.

After a day of rest, Curtis and Price again set off for Mount Shuksan. This time they descended directly into the valley of Swift Creek and climbed what they called Shuksan Ridge, from which they could look across another valley at a cascading glacier. They were undoubtedly near Lake Ann, though they do not mention a lake in their narrative, looking across the valley of Shuksan Creek at what would be named Upper Curtis Glacier. They descended again, going southward along the base of the mountain's west face. Climbing over talus and moraine, they followed a goat trail up slabby rock and gully to timberline part way up the ridge. As the day ended the place felt eerie.

> Sunset found us on a spur at timberline, the lower world lost in the haze from forest fires. The ridges of the mountain disappeared in the smoke below and we felt that our camp was suspended above the world. Across the valley the rounded shoulder of a foothill was visible while outlined in the west was the mighty dome of Baker like some fairy creation in the heavens, rather than a mountain of the earth. Its foothills were gone and the haze softened the icy slopes behind which the sun was setting.[5]

After a cold night, they continued up rock and snow until "before us stretched the great snowfields that cover the main plateau."[6] Sulphide Glacier lay before them. To the east rose lesser pinnacles, with the North Cascades jiggling the horizon beyond. The glacier rose gradually to the summit spire, and soon they were climbing its rock. Climbing was easier than it looked, and soon they were on the summit.

Nothing indicated that anyone had preceded them to the summit – no cairn, tobacco can, or any of the usual marks men leave on mountain tops. They built a cairn, took photographs, basked in the warm sun, and drank in the view. Baker loomed before them to the west. The eastern horizon was a jumble of hundreds of peaks, enough to challenge them for a lifetime. Joe Morovits would later claim that he had made the first ascent of Shuksan, and he may well have. The mountain rose from his back doorstep, and his adventures on Mount Baker certainly indicate he could have made the climb. His story was that he climbed the peak while prospecting and, not thinking it a very significant achievement, had not bothered to leave a mark. Joe may have made the first ascent, but he couldn't prove his claim, so Curtis and Price are credited with the achievement and memorialized with glaciers on the mountain named for them.

John A. Lee and Rodney Glisan meanwhile decided they wanted to climb Baker again. Lee, a former president of the Mazamas, once a school teacher in Blaine and then a Portland attorney, had climbed Boulder Glacier years before with Morovits and may have wished to show his friend Glisan the sights farther up the mountain. Glisan was also a Portland attorney and

Asahel Curtis (left) and Montelius Price (below) on the summit of Mount Shuksan, 1906.

avid amateur photographer (he would amass 147 photo albums, no small feat in those days). The two men, accompanied by a Professor Gleason, set off out Ptarmigan Ridge for another attempt on the big one.

As the trio traversed around Coleman Peak, they dropped down into the gorge of Rainbow Creek rather than continue out the ridge to the glaciers, as they had done previously. Crossing the creek, they struggled up the steep southern wall of the gorge, managing only to make it out of the gorge and onto the ridge beyond by nightfall. They had dropped several thousand feet before winning back half of it on their ascent.

Next morning they descended the ridge, which was in fact a wide plateau – known today as Lava Divide – looking for a way to get onto Mount Baker proper. Their problem was that between them and their route lay another gorge, the bottom of which was the much crevassed lower end of the Park Glacier. They could get to this glacier, but it was overhung by massive ice walls above a band of cliffs which calved thundering avalanches onto Park Glacier's lower surface.

The three men continued down Lava Divide, again losing elevation until they came to a meadow on the eastern edge, where a waterfall dropped down to Park Creek below the snout of the glacier. Professor Gleason looked over the edge. He noted that a thousand-foot descent would be necessary, followed by an eight-thousand-foot climb to the summit, and decided he would stay in the luxurious meadow.

Glisan and Lee, young, ambitious and brash, decided they were up to the task and left everything but light lunch, rope and ice axe with the professor (coats and sweaters as well). They dropped off the ridge down to the creek, crossed it and started upward. By noon they had made remarkable progress, gaining five thousand feet, and had stopped for lunch on Boulder Cleaver. Finding to their dismay that they had left most of their lunch behind, they ate what they had and turned upward again.

The ground was familiar to Lee, but above the cleaver the glacier was heavily crevassed. Travel was extremely slow requiring almost seven hours to negotiate the upper part of the mountain. At 6:45 they signed the recently placed Mazama summit register. Confident of a quick descent they turned immediately downward, but all did not go as anticipated.

> . . . we soon had difficulty retracing our path, which we must do, or otherwise be pocketed in the interlacing crevasses. Lee let his alpenstock slip, and it disappeared in the gloom. Fortunately it was recovered, but valuable time passed, and soon all trace of our track was lost and we were obliged to stop where we were and wait for the moon to aid us. It was somewhat wearisome waiting, having

Climbers solving a route-finding problem on a glacier high on the mountain.

no shelter on the glacier and no rocks to rest on. We crept below the surface of the glacier into a shallow crevasse, but the night-breeze followed us, and as we had no coats or sweaters to keep us warm, we had to act like King George and his men, go down hill a little way and then up again.[7]

Fortunately the night was mild and they survived. "After the lapse of several centuries Dawn appeared" wrote Glisan afterward, and they wasted no time on the downward track.[8]

Once on Boulder Cleaver, Glisan and Lee decided they could save themselves a lot of trouble by traversing Park Glacier above Park Cliffs, then simply drop down to Lava Divide. This was a good idea, but they were turned back by crevasses and forced to return to their original route. As they stood again on Boulder Cleaver, they could see their friend Gleason across the divide, not so far away, and even hear his shouts. Exhausted and hungry, they descended once more down to Park Creek. Food and rest, they thought, would soon be theirs.

The warm weather, which had favored them overnight, now frustrated them. Park Creek was a roaring torrent, fed by rapid snowmelt and glacial runoff. They could not cross and were forced to follow the stream up to where it emerges from beneath the glacier. Using the snout of ice as a bridge, they reached the north side of the stream, then struggled for hours on the north canyon wall. Finally, thirteen hours after exchanging shouts with Professor Gleason, they stumbled, in the dark, into their camp. Glisan and Lee had been on their feet for forty hours. They had eaten very little, traveled many miles, and gained and lost more than eleven thousand feet of elevation. What they thought would be a quick run up the mountains had turned into an epic.

Their work was not over yet; next morning they had to travel twelve rugged miles back to Camp Sholes, only to find horses packed and everyone ready to go home. With barely a rest, the climbers joined the long march back to Sumas for the train ride home to Portland. Glisan and Lee were the first to bivouac near the summit since Coleman and Bennett had done so forty years earlier. They showed tremendous endurance in their four-day trip and made the most of the Mazama outing, succeeding on two strenuous multiday ascents of the peak. Most of the Mazamas, to their irritation, had not touched the summit.

The Mazama outing was the beginning of a new mountaineering era in Mount Baker's history. The group was by far the largest ever to travel into the region for recreation. The outing brought together men and women with climbing experience and ambition, and increasing numbers of such people would try to climb ever more difficult routes on the peak. A new access route

The Mountaineers near the summit, 1908.

was opened to the mountain, and mountaineers thoroughly explored areas visited in the past only briefly by Indians and prospectors. The trip was highly successful from both a recreational and mountaineering standpoint, and participants' descriptions of fun and adventure, published in various magazines, motivated many others to come to Mount Baker. The Mazamas would return in 1909 and many times thereafter.

The other major Northwest climbing club – The Mountaineers from Seattle – came to Mount Baker in 1908. The Mountaineers were formed when a group of Seattle Mazamas decided in 1906 to establish its own organization. The Mountaineers grew rapidly and adopted the approach of the Mazamas, sponsoring an annual outing as the highlight of the year. The 1908 outing was to Mount Baker and was not quite the small army the Mazamas had been – fifty Mountaineers made the trip. Asahel Curtis, L.A. Nelson and John Best, Jr., the outing's three leaders, had made a reconnaissance into the Baker Lake region early in the summer – the eastern side would be the group's object. They spent ten days locating the trail that would have to be

The Mountaineers descending eastern slope of Mount Baker, 1908.

built to timberline, selecting the campsites and arranging for pack animals. They probably visited Joe Morovits and enlisted whatever assistance he was willing and able to provide. Since they would be bringing in thirty-two pack animals and a cow along with the fifty climbers, a substantial trail would be essential. The cow would be slaughtered at base camp to provide fresh meat.

Most of the group arrived by train at Baker (now Concrete) on July 18. They immediately set out up the trail toward Baker Lake and two miles along found their advance party. Camp was all set up for them, the fire was roaring, and dinner was waiting. Next morning, aroused by a bugle call, they set off on the twelve-mile hike to Baker Lake. From the lake they traveled Joe Morovits' trail, then over the seven miles to new trail their group had built until they reached timberline. Conditions were not ideal there, so they continued on another mile before finally establishing base camp for the climb, which they called Mountaineer Camp. The unfortunate cow was duly slaughtered, the horses tethered; the group settled down to enjoy themselves.

This group was not pioneering new ground as the Mazamas had two years before. They were at the base of Boulder Ridge, below Boulder

Glacier. Joe Morovits had hiked and climbed all over the area. Various parties had climbed this side, many led by Joe. The greatest contribution of The Mountaineers outing was the trail it opened up to Boulder Ridge. All previous parties had struggled with the steep and heavily forested approach. After The Mountaineers, even cows could make the trip.

Camp established, the group enjoyed a mountaineering class on the snow. Curtis and other experienced climbers showed the novices rudiments of climbing technique. The next day forty-two members of the party climbed to six thousand feet and explored the glaciers. They got a feel for the terrain and surveyed the difficulties of the climbing route to the summit. The summit attempt would come at dawn.

Their early-morning start was thwarted by a storm. For two days wind and rain buffeted the camp. Clouds draped themselves over the glaciers creating white-out conditions. Climbing was out of the question. Campfire and camaraderie were the order of the day until on the third day the weather cleared. Much to the surprise of the comfortable Mountaineers, a party of cold, wet, bedraggled but relieved climbers came down Boulder Ridge into their camp. Led by Charles Finley Easton, this group had traversed the mountain and spent three uncomfortable nights near the summit in the storm.

Charles Finley Easton

Climbers cross the crevasse in which two days earlier the Easton–Sprague party spent the night while waiting out a storm.

The "official" Mountaineers climb was made up Boulder Ridge and Boulder Glacier. Thirty-nine people made the straightforward and uneventful ascent. Several large crevasses near the summit required care, but everyone negotiated them successfully. The outing was judged a great success by all involved, a "conquest" according to the trip's historian, Lulie Nettleton, who used military metaphor throughout her description of the outing.[9]

The real story of this "Mountaineer" period on the mountain was that of Easton and his rain-soaked companions. Charles Finley Easton had been with the Mazama party in 1906 but had failed to make the summit. In 1908 he planned a climb to coincide with The Mountaineers' visit. He and his companions would make a leisurely approach up Glacier Creek and Grouse Ridge, then climb to the summit and spend a couple of days camped there. He hoped to be there when Curtis and his group arrived and greet them on "his" mountain. By 1908 Easton was passionately interested in all facets of

Mount Baker. He was not yet its official historian and would not assume that title until formation of the Mount Baker Club in 1911, but he had begun his systematic and thorough study of Koma Kulshan.

While The Mountaineers' caravan made its way to base camp, Easton and three other climbers came up the mountain from the west. All went well until they neared the summit, where a strong wind began to blow. Clouds built rapidly, and the four suddenly found themselves in a dangerous situation. They were wet with perspiration after climbing in the hot sun and were rapidly chilled by the damp, cold wind. Two members of the party were particularly affected, both physically and emotionally, by the ordeal.

Fortunately, they were near a cleaver of rock just below the summit and found a spacious moat between the rock and glacier. Moats form in summer when rock absorbs the warmth of the sun and melts any snow in contact with it. Easton and another strong climber descended into the moat and dug a snow cave into which the whole party crowded. Down in the moat they were out of the howling wind and in relative comfort could enlarge their cave. Eventually they got their stove going, melted snow for water and even dried some of their clothing. The four passed a fairly comfortable night in their cave.

Next morning conditions seemed to have improved slightly. They climbed upward, reaching the summit and emerging into cold and windy sunlight. They were in the midst of a wind-tossed sea of cloud. Only the summits of Mount Shuksan to the east and Mount Rainier to the south were visible. The biting cold soon drove them off the summit and back to their cave, where they debated the next move.

A return trip down the way they had come did not appeal to them. Several very steep and broken sections of glacier had been climbed, and Easton was not certain he could retrace his way down the glacier in the storm. Conditions were again terrible, cloud and snow so thick that it was difficult, sometimes impossible, to distinguish snow from air. They easily could have walked off the edge of a crevasse or steep wall without seeing it. An alternative was to complete the traverse and go down the eastern side to where The Mountaineers were camped. Though unknowns and severe conditions might prevail that way too, Easton reasoned that he and his party might soon meet The Mountaineers climbing up. Easton also knew that if they could reach Boulder Cleaver, which extended high on Baker's eastern side, they could follow it down. The plan was a gamble, but the odds seemed better to the east than on the broad glacial expanses to the west and south.

Leaving the ice cave after a second night, they had to traverse northeast and then descend. The steep slopes of the crater forced them upward before they could go down. Slowly they groped their way downward, cautiously negotiating the bergshcrund at the top of Boulder Glacier and initially

MT. BAKER VIEWS—MAZAMA SERIES—THE SUMMIT JUST ABOVE.
COPYRIGHTED 1906, BY CHARLES FINLEY EASTON.

Mazamas taking a break below the summit.

steep upper slopes. Soon they found themselves in a heavily crevassed section of the glacier. Visibility remained near zero as they spent the remaining daylight hours slowly threading their way downward among crevasses. As night again fell they were blocked from further downward progress by an immense crevasse. The dream of a warm campfire at timberline faded as they faced another cold bivouac.

Casting about for some way to get out of the wind, they found a crevasse in which a large block of snow was wedged, providing a level platform out of the storm. After gathering flat stones from a nearby cleaver and laying them on the snow platform, the party descended into the crevasse for the night. Easton describes the trials that followed.

> One of the most disagreeable features of this night's lodging in cold storage was the chilly current of air that rose from the unknown depths of the crevasse like the draft of some immense flue. . . . That night in the crevasse every few minutes the ice would snap with a sharp, short twing accompanied by a perceptible movement, never more than the smallest fraction of an inch but an unmistakable slipping, a movement which would probably not be noticed from the surface above. The whole field of ice seemed to be on the move. . . . In our refrigeration . . . we could hear the cracking of the glaciers for miles and miles through on the opposite side of the mountain, and faint rumblings, which may have been due to the grinding of the ice upon the rocks or it may have come from the bowels of the earth where Pluto is working up another volcanic eruption.[10]

As dawn approached, the weather improved and warmed markedly. They crawled out of their chilly refuge to see Boulder Cleaver not far away. Easton had made his traverse, the first on record, though all had not gone as planned. The four had been smart and fortunate and survived conditions that might have killed them. They went down the ridge and before long were luxuriating in dry clothing, with hot tea, a roaring fire, and The Mountaineers.

The Mazamas decided to come back to Mount Baker for their annual outing in 1909. This time they would visit yet another side of the mountain and hoped it would provide an opportunity for more members of the group to climb to the summit than had been able to do so on the steep northeast side three years earlier. Once again they contacted the Forest Service for assistance with access and received plenty of help. There was a rough wagon road a short distance up the Middle Fork of the Nooksack River and a trail five miles to the Washington National Forest Boundary. The Forest Service had built their Deming Ranger Station near the boundary in 1908. To reach the southern slopes of Mount Baker, it would be necessary to extend the trail eleven miles beyond the ranger station to timberline.

Forest Supervisor C.H. Park was in favor of extending the trail, but the Forest Service could not do it alone. Its budget and staff were small. Awareness of Mount Baker as a tourist attraction and of all the economic benefits that it could bring was increasing in local communities. The citizens of Deming made contributions for what came to be called the Deming Trail. The Bellingham Chamber of Commerce pitched in for construction of foot logs and bridges. Rangers Joe Ridley and Carl Bell surveyed the trail and supervised the work. The trail was ready when sixty Mazamas (club membership was smaller now that The Mountaineers had split off) arrived early in August.

Several members of the group who lived in Bellingham arranged for a welcome and entertainment in that community. Then a long file of climbers and packhorses headed up the trail assisted by Rangers Ridley and Bell, who showed them a good campsite. An open, parklike area at timberline was selected for base camp – Camp Gorman – and parties set out to explore the area. One group immediately came upon a beautiful region of subalpine meadows which they named, predictably, Mazama Park – "fifty acres of sunshine, red and white heather, rare alpine flowers and hungry butterflies."[11] Another party, led by veteran John A. Lee, wandered high on the mountain exploring the glaciers. Names had not yet been assigned to Baker's southern glaciers, and they wanted to determine how many glaciers there were before they named them. Glacier edges were difficult to locate high on the mountain, for the southern slope seemed incased in one massive sheet of ice. By examining streams running from the base of the glacial masses and configurations of ice at their lower ends, Lee's group decided there were several glaciers.

When Lee's party came back to camp after their glacial explorations, they held a campfire for the whole group.

> One night, the red glow of the Mazama camp-fire fell upon a group of mountaineers in khaki and corduroy sitting cross-legged before the fire drying their spiked boots – scarlet sweaters and bandannas catching the shifting glow – while three score eager sun-browned faced were upturned to a man in rough mountain garb; a man for whom the arctic snows that crowned Mt. Baker had perpetual fascination, whose zest for exploration had on a former occasion brought him into the very jaws of death there on that crystal dome cutting the heavens. . . . No man had given himself

114

with such unquenchable zeal to the study and exploration of this peak as Charles F. Easton, who stood among his fellow club members recounting the changes he had noted in this "Great White Watcher" of the Indians. . . . As he talked, we resolved that for no one else should our newly explored glacier be named.[12]

We can imagine Easton, a wiry Bellingham businessman of fifty-one years, waxing enthusiastic about the mountain that obsessed him. He told the group how, in 1906, he had been sketching the mountain from far to the west, looking at it through a telescope, when massive avalanches came off the western side, completely changing its appearance. Ice and rock slid off at the precise moment of the great San Francisco earthquake, a remarkable coincidence. Easton speculated there might have been some connection between these geological events (a speculation to which geologists today lend no credence). He told them the history of the mountain as he knew it and all that he knew about glaciers, which was considerable. And, of course, he described in detail his epic traverse of the mountain the previous summer.

Easton was born in Michigan in 1858, raised in Iowa, and educated as an engineer at Valparaiso University in Indiana. He enjoyed a varied career as teacher, mining engineer, geologist, bridge-builder, assayer, inventor and jeweler. He had been granted the first x-ray tube patent in the United States. He taught himself jewelry artisanship and moved west to Wallace, Idaho, where he opened a jewelry store and rose to prominence in the community, eventually becoming a state senator.

Wallace was not a very stable town in the nineteenth century, and his tenure there ended when striking miners blew up a mill and paralyzed the town with violence. Easton moved to Seattle and then, in 1900, to Bellingham, where he opened another jewelry store. Soon he embarked on his studies of Mount Baker. He joined the Mazamas and was on Mount Baker every year, becoming a recognized expert on the peak. When, in 1911, a group of local leaders formed the Mount Baker Club to promote development of the Mount Baker region, Easton was named historian of the group. For the next twenty years, until his death in 1931, Easton studied and wrote about the mountain extensively. He surveyed it, preparing a map that later amazed United States Geological Survey topographers with its accuracy and detail. He collected material about the mountain in a huge scrapbook, which became Exhibit A in the push to make the Mount Baker region a national park. He was chief lobbyist in Washington, D.C. for this proposal, which was ultimately side-tracked by international events. So it was perhaps more appropriate than anyone realized at the time that the Mazamas in 1909 named their new glacier for Charles Finley Easton.

A large summit party, typical of the era.

The 1909 Mazama outing's most significant contributions to Mount Baker's history occurred more around the campfires than on the slopes. In addition to naming Easton Glacier, they also named Deming Glacier, in tribute to the town that had assisted with the trail construction that made the outing possible. They named a buttress of the Black Buttes for their leader John A. Lee – Lee Promontory; creeks were named for the helpful rangers Joe Ridley and Carl Bell. At one campfire a resolution was offered that Mount Baker, Mount Shuksan and the Sisters Range be "forever preserved as a national park."[13] The idea had first been tossed about at campfires of the 1906 outing but had come to nothing. The resolution in 1909 was the real beginning of an effort to preserve (and promote) Mount Baker and its surrounding peaks.

Between campfires the Mazamas did climb the mountain. Several parties went up the Easton and Deming glaciers; some enthusiasts climbed the mountain two and even three times. The "official" ascent departed for the summit on August 11. Thirty-eight climbers ultimately reached the top.

Ropes were not uncoiled for the official climb. President Gorman announced that they would make this ascent without the life-line of a climb-

ing rope. Rope-handling with big groups was too much trouble, and this side of the mountain seemed benign. No mishaps occurred, but the incident is indicative of the increasingly light regard people had at the time for the threat of hidden crevasses, an attitude that would cause problems in years to come.

The Mazama climb was a great success. Before they headed back down the Deming Trail, fifty-four of sixty people in camp reached the summit. No difficult climbing was done, no new routes pushed up, but the 1906 "failure" was erased when so many Mazamas walked upon the summit snows. A new region of the mountain had been extensively explored, and the new trail opened a marvelous alpine playground for generations to come.

Before the Mazamas came in 1906, all parties had been small. They had quite a struggle to make their climbs. The region was wilderness, with few trails, and approaches to the mountain often proved as taxing as the climb above timberline. The three club climbs opened up Mount Baker both physically and psychologically. Trails were built, and more than one hundred people climbed onto the summit glacier. The 1908 and 1909 climbs were so uneventful that people began to think of Mount Baker, at least over the commonly climbed routes, as an easy climb. This view would soon have consequences.

Two other ascents during the years dominated by the clubs should be mentioned. Many climbs were made each year after 1909; most of them accomplished nothing new of significance. But two climbs are important because they, too, indicate new attitudes about the mountain. In 1907 Joe Morovits once again led a group to the summit up the Boulder Glacier. Six young men from Bellingham helped Joe with his haying so that he would be free to make the climb. Once there were under way the group climbed with speed, making the ascent from timberline in five and a half hours. They had so much time to kill on the summit that they waltzed over and climbed Sherman Peak, claiming the first ascent (though it probably was not). They returned to the summit of Baker, which required more climbing, then descended to snowline in one hour and twelve minutes. Descriptions of their trip emphasize its speed.

In 1908 another local party left Bellingham on July 21. They were back in town, having reached the summit, in three days, 15 hours and 15 minutes. The fact that they recorded their time so exactly indicates that parties were now vying with each other for speed records. This racing mentality shows that people were thinking of Mount Baker very differently than had their predecessors. This new view would reach its apex in a few years – with the Mount Baker Marathons.

7

The Marathons

Mount Baker is getting a formal introduction to the people of our Republic. This mountain and its immediate environs are deserving of improvement and development for its scenic value. It is the object of the Mount Baker Club to continue these marathons as long as they may be beneficial in stirring up active interest and co-operation in the building of roads and better trails which will aid in opening up the fascinating features of the WONDERLAND.
— Charles Finley Easton, 1911

Perhaps the most remarkable chapter in the story of Mount Baker is that of the Marathons. The idea of a race to the summit was the brainchild of the Mount Baker Club, a group of businessmen in Bellingham who organized to promote tourism and development in the Mount Baker region. Their inspiration came from the example of Mount Rainier which had become a national park in 1899 and was rapidly becoming a tourist attraction of great benefit to business in the communities near it. The Mount Baker Club set out to draw the nation's attention to its mountain with the goal of making it a similar tourist attraction. An editorial in the local newspaper summarized the motivation and aspiration of the group.

> There is no better advertising feature than the mountain and island scenery hereabouts. If these things were brought to the attention of the pleasure-seeking Americans from the eastern and middle states there would be a mighty stream of travel this way. And these men and women are usually looking for investments and change of location while traveling about the country on pleasure bent. . . . .[1]

In 1911 the Mount Baker Club thought of a gimmick that might start the flow of people and money – a Mount Baker Marathon.

Poster promoting the 1912 Mount Baker Marathon.

Appropriately enough, the race would begin at the Chamber of Commerce in downtown Bellingham. Racers would have their choice of conveyance to one of two trails up the mountain. One option was a special train up the Bellingham Bay and British Columbia Railroad forty-four miles to Glacier on the North Fork of the Nooksack River which would get them to the Glacier Trail route to the summit. Or, they could drive by car twenty-six miles to Heisler's Ranch on the Middle Fork and run sixteen miles up the Middle Fork on the Deming Trail to the summit. The latter course was longer but supposedly of gentler grade. The race would pit not only the men but the machines they used against one another. The two trails would be competing as well: the people of Glacier would build the trail up Glacier Creek, and they wanted to prove that their trail was the best way up the mountain. An influx of mountain climbers and hikers would, after all, be very good for their new but growing community. The Deming Trail would benefit that community and they were committed to improving it. The race was not just good advertising and an athletic competition – it was a test of technologies and community spirit and organization as well.

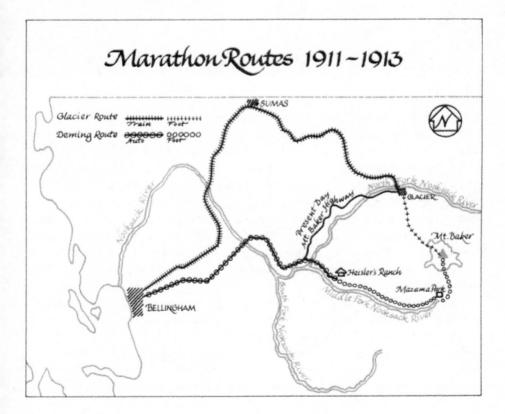

Fourteen lean and determined competitors lined up for the start of the first race at 10 p.m. on Thursday, August 10, 1911. The late evening start would allow runners to climb the mountain at night when the snow was hard, which presumably would be easier and safer than during the day. The weather was ideal. Parties from Deming and Glacier had been working on the trails and reported them in prime condition. Judges were poised at timberline, ready to climb to the summit to check the racers who got that far. Each racer carried a certificate to be countersigned by judges at the summit and at the finish back in Bellingham. Fifteen "guards" were stationed at intervals along the trails to discourage cheating. Thousands of spectators reportedly lined the streets for the start.

At the bark of the starting gun, six racers roared off in automobiles, probably the first stripped-down hotrods ever to travel Bellingham streets. Drivers took the first corner on two wheels and roared down a straightaway and across railroad tracks, barely beating the train carrying the other eight racers. The crowd cheered them on, then went home to bed or settled down to other diversions to pass the time until the finish. No one knew how long

Joe Galbraith near the end of the run at Heisler's Ranch.

the wait would be – the record for the round-trip from Bellingham to the summit and back (insofar as people were beginning to record such feats) was thirty-three hours.

The train reached Glacier in fifty-three minutes and eight racers hit the trail. They faced a round-trip of approximately twenty-eight miles, half of it uphill in the dark with an elevation gain of some 9800 feet (an average of 347 feet to the mile, though the grade was certainly not even all the way and very steep in a few places). Among the Glacier racers was Harvey Haggard, a woodsman and logger from Glacier. Haggard wore light clothing and tennis shoes for the trail run to timberline, where he would change to caulked logging boots for the run across the Coleman and Deming glaciers.

The men in automobiles reached Heisler's Ranch well before the train arrived in Glacier. Jumping out, they stripped off the heavy clothing they wore to protect them from the wind chill of their speedy ride in open cars. They faced a thirty-two mile run, with an elevation gain like that of their opponents, but the grade of their route was easier for most of the way. Their final climb up the Easton and Deming glaciers would be steep.

The competitive field was narrowed considerably by the time the runners reached the glaciers. All but six had succumbed to injury, exhaustion, or common sense. The first runner to reach the top was N.B. Randall of Glacier, coming up over the Glacier Trail route. Harvey Haggard was close behind. Joe Galbraith was the first to reach the judges by the Deming Trail.

As the race progressed a strong, cold wind began to blow. The judges on the summit endured it as long as they could, then retreated to a protected spot on the rim of the crater. This became a problem for Turner Riddle who came up the Deming Trail. "When I got to the top the judges were blue with cold," said Riddle.

> I knew I was beat, but wanted to reach the summit. The judges took forty minutes off my time and sent me back again. It was not my fault I did not get to the top. My carbide light gave out and for ten miles I stumbled along the trail in the dark. I held a candle which lasted me four miles, but this did not give much light.[2]

Five racers registered at the summit before the judges were forced down out of the wind.

Joe Galbraith boards "Betsy" for the dash to Bellingham with his driver, Hugh Diehl.

Harvey Haggard (in robe), grim because his train derailed after hitting a bull.

Harvey Haggard was running well. After checking in on the summit behind Randall, he steadily gained on him and beat him to the train by several hundred feet. The rule was that the first man to the train got it for the final leg back to Bellingham. So Haggard roared off down the track leaving poor Randall, who had run a great race, to cool his heels in Glacier.

Haggard's dreams of glory were premature. A few miles down the track the speeding train with its engine, tender, and single car hit a large bull that was astride the track, derailed and tipped onto its side. Haggard was more than thirty miles from the coveted finish line. No one was hurt. The crew tried to call a speeder, a small gasoline-powered railroad maintenance vehicle, but could not get one quickly enough for the determined Haggard. He caught a buggy on the road nearby, and the driver lashed his horse at a run for thirty minutes. Haggard commandeered a saddle horse when the beleaguered buggy horse gave out. A few miles down the road at Kendall, he was thrown from that horse into the dust. Remarkably uninjured by all of these mishaps, he was then picked up by an automobile, which finally carried him without further serious mishap to the finish.

Meanwhile Joe Galbraith made good time down the Deming Trail. His Ford and its driver, H.W. Diehl, were waiting for him at Heisler's for the race

Joe Galbraith: "Now we're in real trouble, Hugh."

to Bellingham. Diehl's car, "Betsy," reached more than fifty miles per hour on the straight stretches, quite a pace in those days. Galbraith registered at the Chamber of Commerce twelve hours and twenty-eight minutes after the start. Haggard, despite all of his mishaps, came in just thirty-two minutes later to take second place. Turner Riddle finished third. The Deming Trail and the automobile had won. Galbraith collected the first prize, a whopping sum of one hundred dollars and a buffalo robe.

The first race had been a great success. Thousands had witnessed it. The advertising potential was clear. The Mount Baker Club, editors of local newspapers and the Bellingham Chamber of Commerce were certain that they had struck a bonanza. An editorial in the *American Reveille*, Bellingham's leading newspaper at the time, expressed this view in July of the next year as the community prepared for the second race.

> The Mount Baker Marathon, with its attendant features, continues to grow in importance as a great Western festival. Started only a year ago it is already well known in almost every city on the

Pacific Coast and the news of the great event is gradually creeping into all parts of the United States. . . . The fact that it is spectacular and entirely without parallel in the world, is a decided advertising advantage. By all means the Marathons should be made an annual event. It is typically Western, something that stirs a red-blooded generation and one of the biggest assets of Bellingham.[3]

An annual event it would be. The 1912 race was scheduled to start at 11 p.m. on July 24.

Several rule changes were made to improve the race. The 1911 race had been open only to entrants from the three Northwest Washington counties. A new rule opened it to runners from anywhere in the world, organizers hoping world-class runners would enter. A second change was made to avoid a collision of cars and train at the crossing near the start. Autos were given a one-minute head start. Racers were encouraged to have attendants at any and all points in the race, as long as these attendants did not transport the racer. "The committee recommends that all contestants be accompanied by at least one other person above the timberline."[4] As impractical as this was, it indicated concern for the safety of the racers among the crevasses on the upper mountain. This time the judges would erect shelters on the summit and stay there the night of the race. Finally, gasoline speeders would be provided for the second, third and fourth men down the Glacier Trail. Four places would

Judges erecting their summit shelter, 1912.

Spent marathon runner reaches trailhead.

win cash prizes; the first prize was five hundred dollars, a very large sum for the times. Race officials hoped the purse would attract some outstanding competitors.

One problem with the first marathon as a spectator event was that once the racers left the start, little was known of them until they neared the finish. To follow their progress, officials decided to string a telephone line from Glacier, where it could be connected to an existing line, to the summit of the mountain along the race course. Phones could be installed every two miles over this fourteen-mile line, and progress up the Glacier Trail could be monitored. The Deming Trail was too long for such a setup, though plans were made to run a line at least to Mazama Park along that trail.

A full program of events was planned for the three-day festival, and the large purse did attract some accomplished athletes: Jimmy Fitzgerald of Calgary, Alberta, winner of many long-distance races and a Canadian Olympian in 1908; Paul Westerlund of San Francisco, a twenty-seven-year-old marathon champion and immigrant from Finland; Victor Norman, a thirty-seven-year-old veteran of many long-distance races. Local entrants included "Johnny" Magnusson, a tough timber cruiser who had raced the previous year, Harvey Haggard and Turner Riddle, determined to better their 1911 showings, and Victor Galbraith, cousin of the great Joe. But Joe himself had broken a shoulder in an auto crash near Heisler's Ranch while training only two weeks before the second race. He would have to sit this one out. All of these aspirants were on the mountain for weeks before the race, training and plotting the best course among the crevasses.

Telephone line was strung to timberline; remaining wire would be stretched to the top just before the race. Three hundred small American flags were carried up to mark the trails. The judges climbed to the summit and erected their shelters. They carried up a red lantern and an American flag. The lantern would guide racers who reached the summit before dawn, the flag those who came after daylight. They also carried "red fire powder," which they would light at the appointed starting times in hope that spectators in Bellingham would be able to see the other end of the course.

As race day approached, a carnival atmosphere enveloped the whole region. Three U.S. Navy cruisers steamed in and anchored in Bellingham Bay. The Sells-Floto Circus spread its tents. Balloon ascensions competed with war canoe races and other water events for the attention of the crowds, estimated by some as high as sixty thousand (more realistically probably fifteen to twenty thousand). Thousands of yards of green and white bunting, the colors of the Mount Baker Club, decorated the city, and American flags flew everywhere. Judges, guides, spectators, and attendants all stationed themselves on the mountain.

Crowds gathered; machines to carry the runners were given their final inspections and lined up for the start. Then, to the shock of everyone involved, summit judges J. Will Collins and Nathan L. Davis called over the Glacier Trail telephone to say that they had been turned back at timberline by a raging storm. Conditions on the mountain were terrible. Several feet of snow had fallen up high and below snowline the trails were torrents. The road from Deming to trailhead at Heisler's Ranch was a quagmire impassable to automobiles. Collins and Davis refused "to send men to their deaths." The race would have to be postponed, and one wonders today how preparations had reached so close to the beginning of the race without anyone reporting the change in the mountain weather. Perhaps race officials simply couldn't bring themselves to believe a bad forecast.

Though the centerpiece of the marathon festival was removed, everyone basking in the fine weather west of the mountain on the edge of Bellingham Bay enjoyed themselves. The Navy ships hosted thousands of visitors. All manner of land and water races were run, and festival promoters were pleased despite the loss of the race. Meanwhile, the storm continued to pound the high country. We can imagine the racer's disappointment; some were on a tight schedule and would miss the race when it was rescheduled.

On Saturday the 27th Mount Baker appeared from the clouds. New snow draped the summit, but weather reports were good. The race would be run on the 31st. Postponement had reduced the number of racers from sixteen to nine, and these stalwarts lined up to go. Judges reported from the saddle below the summit (as far as the telephone line finally reached) that the weather was again poor but much better than it had been. The starting gun was fired at 11 p.m. and off they went. Three roared away in automobiles for the Deming Trail, the rest on the train to Glacier.

Judges camped in their shelters on the summit as originally planned. They erected their lantern and flag on a pole, but the driving mist thwarted all attempts to light the lantern. Visibility was very poor, but the three hundred flags placed along both routes helped the racers greatly. Even with flags, though, some had problems finding their way.

Without lantern light, judges shouted constantly to guide the racers to them in the darkness and mist. At about 4:30 their shouts were answered and the bedraggled form of Paul Westerlund staggered out of the mist. Coming up the Glacier Trail, he had lost his way after reaching the saddle a thousand feet below the summit. He eventually relocated the flags but was near collapse when he reached the judges. His wet clothes were freezing to him. He wore light canvas shoes with spikes on the soles, and his arms were bare to the elbows. The judges tried to warm him and gave him a cup of hot coffee before he disappeared back into the gloom.

A few minutes after Westerlund departed, Joe Frankoviz arrived in better shape and shouted to the judges that they had better go down and help Harvey Haggard, who had collapsed on the upper part of the Roman Wall. As they started for him, Haggard came into view, his name well fitting his condition. The judges wondered if he could (and should) continue the race, but he seemed to recover quickly with the hot coffee and the realization that the rest of the race was downhill. He was soon off in pursuit of Westerlund and Frankoviz. Victor Galbraith, last of the Glacier Trail runners still in competition, checked in.

Meanwhile Johnny Magnusson and Turner Riddle were battling their way up the Deming Trail. Hugh Galbraith, another cousin of Joe and Victor and the third racer on this route, dropped out at timberline. Riddle and Magnusson registered on the summit four minutes apart but almost an hour behind those who had come up the other route. The two raced back down the mountain and jogged to their automobiles shoulder to shoulder after thirty-two miles of racing.

Paul Westerlund had a ten minute lead on his closest rival when he checked off the summit, but on the downward trail he gradually lost ground to Frankoviz, Haggard and Galbraith, who all passed him three miles from Glacier. They did not realize that they were witness to a remarkable display of grit and courage, for Westerlund had fallen on steep ice on the way up and sustained internal injuries and a broken rib. They thought he was just worn out, as they were. When the leaders passed the two-mile mark, a phone call went down to Glacier informing them that it would likely be a tight finish at the train. The engineer began to build his head of steam, and the conductor and brakeman stretched out a rope at the rear of the coach.

Two racers emerged from the forest, splattered from head to toe with mud, running shoulder to shoulder. Frankoviz seemed to surge ahead. Then Haggard, probably remembering his frustrations of the previous year, summoned a final reserve of energy and just beat him to the rope. They had been racing (running, walking, stumbling, sliding or otherwise moving) for seven hours and thirty-eight minutes. A newspaper reporter described the scene at the train as Haggard and Frankoviz climbed aboard.

> "Wait for Vic," both men murmured, as if with one breath. At that moment Victor Galbraith came dashing into sight down the trail. His stride was long and fast, but he surged from one side of the trail to the other. . . . The Concrete athlete's running suit, which had been snowy white when he left the train, was now fairly reeking with black muck. He, like his rivals, had stumbled and fallen headlong scores of times on the terrific race down the trail.[5]

*Judges Camp at Mazama Lake
1913 Marathon*

While some judges camped on the snow, others enjoyed all the comforts of home.

Race planners had specified that the train was to wait one minute after the first runner reached it. If more than one made it to the train all the better, for they would then have to race the two blocks to the Bellingham Chamber of Commerce Building. Spectators would love it. The racers themselves had other ideas, agreeing that they would place in the order in which they had reached the train. They would jog to the finish in that order to delight the people, but the race was over, at least between them.

The train steamed into Bellingham, this time without tangling with any livestock, thanks to volunteers who patrolled the rails. The three runners tumbled out of the car and made for the finish to the applause of the large crowd. Harvey Haggard checked in with incredible elapsed time of nine hours and fifty-one minutes. The other two were only seconds behind. They had traveled eighty-eight miles by train and roughly twenty-eight miles on foot. The record was lowered by two hours and thirty-seven minutes. All six finishers, the first four of whom had run over the Glacier Trail (Westerlund finished despite his injuries), bettered the previous record.

Despite its postponement the second marathon had been a rousing success, at least in the opinion of most people. Some, however, began to doubt the wisdom of running around on glaciers at night in poor weather. As a promotional stunt the race was unquestionably a success, but it was becoming clear that the racers were pushing themselves to dangerous extremes. Johnny Magnusson lost eleven pounds in his eleven-hour effort. Westerlund had been injured in his fall. Drivers told of runners jogging senselessly past waiting cars at the Deming Trail. Teammates had to catch and carry them to the autos, tying them in their seats so they would not fall from the open cars.

Still, these unusual men showed remarkable recuperative powers. Turner Riddle rode his bicycle twenty miles before and after his marathons. Joe Galbraith went home to do his chores after his win the first year. No one suffered any lasting ill effects from participation in the first two races. Promoters still visualized the race as an every-growing annual event.

The third marathon was scheduled for August 15, 1913. Concern for the welfare of racers grew as more people reflected on the risks revealed by the previous race. More changes were made to make it safer. Runners this time would be required to halt for twelve minutes at snowline to put on warm clothing. When they reached car or train they would change again to dry clothes. The start was scheduled for 5 a.m. so that the race could be run entirely in daylight. Finally, runners would go up one trail and descend the other.

This time there were twelve entrants. All would use both car and train, thereby equalizing the mechanical dimensions of the race. The two previous races had clearly established that the Glacier Trail, while steeper, was the faster way to go. The train ride, while somewhat longer and slower, reduced the distance runners from Glacier had to go. Since everyone would cover the same ground, the 1913 contest would truly be one of human strength and endurance. Nathan L. Davis was again a summit judge, and again he decided at the last minute that the weather was too bad to stage the race. Much new snow had accumulated on the upper mountain, rain was currently falling, and the judges did not dare venture up the mountain to mark the route. This time Davis was in Mazama Park, on the Deming Trail, and after telling race officials back in Bellingham (a phone line was strung on this trail) that the race should be postponed, he, another judge and a Seattle newspaper reporter went back to the Mount Baker Club cabin in Mazama Park to wait out the storm. They were sure the race would be called off. Before long the weather cleared a bit, and the three set off down the trail.

Before they had gone very far they were aghast to see Paul Westerlund, Joe Frankoviz and Lester Vaughn running up the trail toward them. The race was on after all. The two startled judges stopped the runners, told them of

Rescue in 1913.

conditions, that the route was not marked and that no judges were on the mountain to check them in. They advised them to go only over the saddle rather than make the final steep climb to the summit. They then hustled back up the trail and gave the runners what warm clothing they could before they set out up the snow. Racers quickly disappeared up the mountain into the mist.

Marathoners coming up the Glacier Trail, led by Johnny Magnusson, did not know that the judges had instructed racers on the other trail to go only through the saddle. They most likely reached the saddle up the shorter route without meeting Westerlund and the others so proceeded on up to the summit. Magnusson, Victor Norman, Victor Galbraith and A.M. Burnside all found themselves together on the summit with no judges anywhere to be seen. Fog was thick, the wind blowing hard and very cold. The four were concerned because there was no sign of anyone from the Deming side. Burnside agreed to stay a while on the summit to check any others that might come to the top, and the other three started back down the Deming Glacier.

Magnusson had been over the route many times in practice runs and knew the glacier well; he soon left the other two behind. At snowline Davis and his crew, now comprised of members of the runners' support teams and forest ranger Joe Ridley, were watching anxiously. Magnusson passed, then Victor Norman, who told them to watch for Vic Galbraith, who might be in trouble. After a while Burnside appeared out of the fog. The crew asked if he had seen Galbraith. He had not, and he confirmed their fears that Galbraith was not where he should be. Burnside suggested that Vic might have passed around the judges somehow and was on the trail. But Davis, nervous about the whole situation, angrily told Burnside that he doubted that was possible, then immediately dispatched a rescue party up the mountain.

As the three runners had come down the Deming and Easton glaciers, Galbraith had found himself slipping behind. Trying to gain a few feet, he took a shortcut, only to fall forty feet into a hidden crevasse. Miraculously he broke no bones. Finding that he could stand on a snow bridge deep in the crevasse, he jogged gingerly, waving and slapping his arms to stay somewhat warm. Five hours after he descended into his dark glacial den he heard the shouts of his cousin Joe and ranger Ridley, who quickly dropped a rope to him and hauled him up, cold and bruised but none the worse for long-term wear. He had miraculously survived. The rule change requiring the warm clothes helped him as had Victor Norman's feeling that something was wrong. Judge Davis' prompt action and the good luck of the search party in finding the small hole through which Galbraith had fallen all prevented a tragedy. Had Galbraith broken a bone in his fall or been knocked unconscious, he would certainly have perished from hypothermia if not from his injuries.

While all of this was happening on the glacier, Paul Westerlund was running a good race and was first back to Bellingham, in nine hours and thirty-four minutes. He was followed by Frankoviz, then Magnusson. Needless to say all the racers, but especially Magnusson, were upset at the confusion that had rendered the final placing meaningless. Magnusson had gone to the summit — the other two had merely gone over the saddle as they had been instructed. In the end, race officials decided to award first prizes of four hundred dollars to both Magnusson and Westerlund.

The third marathon had been a fiasco and left bitterness and controversy. Judge Davis was furious. He wrote a lengthy letter to the Bellingham *American-Reveille* explaining his view of what had happened. He would, he said, have nothing to do with any future races, since marathon organizers seemed more concerned about the spectators than the racers. Simple luck, he pointed out, had saved Victor Galbraith.

Some contended that Paul Westerlund had not won the race fairly, despite the two first prizes. These doubters suggested that if challenged head-to-head by local runners he would lose. A.M. Burnside challenged Westerlund to a race from Glacier to the summit and back. Burnside was a tough trapper who had given up his chance for prize money when he agreed to wait on the summit for other runners. He was confident that he could win, having led all the way up the Glacier Trail to the summit; Westerlund had come up the other way.

The rematch was run in early September, Burnside leading most of the way, only to be overtaken by Westerlund with just three miles to go. Westerlund's winning time was six hours and two minutes over the twenty-eight-mile course with its 9,700 foot elevation gain (and loss). He certainly dispelled any doubts about his strength, though Burnside later claimed to have had such a bad ankle that his doctor had advised him not to race.

This was the last race up Mount Baker. The Mount Baker Club could not promote an event as risky as the marathon for any reason and certainly not as a publicity stunt. In July, just before the third race, a climber from British Columbia had fallen into a crevasse and died. Victor Galbraith's close call reiterated the message of that misadventure. If the race were continued it would only be a matter of time before a marathon-related death would occur.

Marathon promoters were unrealistic in their belief that people could play games on the mountain's upper slopes. In the years before the first race climbers had been making ever-faster ascents to the summit, and no one was having any great difficulty. Even safety-conscious groups like the Mazamas were going up without ropes. There seemed no great danger and speed-climbing seemed a reasonable thing to do. Still, race promoters knew the dangers if the racers might not. They had hoped that racers would have companions on the glacier; they made rules to reduce hazards; they cautioned racers about specific hazards. But despite their awareness, their enthusiasm and booster-ism overcame their anxieties and common sense. They might do everything they could in advance to make the race safe, but when the pressure to race was on, officials succumbed to enthusiasm rather than caution and sent racers off into dangerous conditions. Storms and hidden crevasses, among other hazards like icy slopes, muddy trails, and even avalanches of fresh snow, were impossible to predict and control. Mount Baker, they found, was a dangerous place, even in the middle of summer. Mountaineers knew this, but they were a small group, a small minority of the Mount Baker Club membership. The Mount Baker Marathon was instructive for many people. Even though the mountain was easily accessible, the climbers experienced and well-trained, their equipment the latest and very best, a climb up a mountain as large as Mount Baker, exposed as it is to fickle mountain weather, is always governed by the vagaries of nature. To deny these vagaries can be an invitation to disaster, and only great luck saved racers and boosters from just such disaster.

In 1972 the marathon served as the inspiration for another race. Over the years since the first marathons there have been proposals to revive the race, but the problem of safety has always scotched the idea. The race initiated in 1972 was again the brainchild of local boosters, but this time it did not involve the high mountain itself. Nordic and alpine skiers, runners, road and mountain bikers, canoeists and sea kayakers, even sailors for a time, have raced from "ski" to "sea" covering eighty miles in a relay descending five thousand feet from the Mount Baker Ski Area to Bellingham Bay. This race is part of a community festival in Bellingham that would warm the hearts of the early Marathon boosters. It usually involves four hundred teams of eight racers. The Ski to Sea Race, too, is subject to the vagaries of weather and presents risks and hazards, but not to the extremes of the high mountain. The canoe leg was cancelled in the 2008 race because of dangerous floodwaters in the Nooksack River, but with modern technology this posed no problem. If the Galbraiths, Harvey Haggard and other Mount Baker Marathon runners could witness today's race, they would think it pretty tame, but surely they would be in the running.

8

Parks, Roads and Resorts: 1913-1930

The natural resources must be developed and preserved for the benefit of the many, and not merely for the profit of a few. We are coming to understand in this country that public action for public benefit has a very much wider field to cover and a much larger part to play than was the case when there were resources enough for everyone.

— Gifford Pinchot, 1910

The years that followed the marathons were relatively quiet for Mount Baker. Climbers continued to visit the mountain in increasing numbers, but the pioneering had been done. For many years after the races, there were no newsworthy ascents. The Forest Service continued to develop its management policies and increase its influence in the area. People in Bellingham continued to regard the mountain as a great commercial asset and sought ways to take advantage of it. Their efforts to open and develop the area are the story of the decade following the marathons.

When the Mount Baker club was organized in 1911 to promote use of scenic resources of the Mount Baker region, its purposes were clearly stated in its constitution. Foremost was the following:

> The objects of this organization shall be to make known and draw public attention to the unrivaled scenic beauties of the MT. BAKER REGION; to establish camps or resorts which will be available to mountain climbers, tourists and those seeking outdoor enjoyment and recreation; to construct trails and highways and to secure national, state, county and public aid for the construction of such roadways; and, to collect photographic and engineering data,

Early Forest Service packtrain.

general history, scientific, botanic, geologic, and other information pertaining to said region.

The club's first big effort to pursue these "objects" was the staging of the marathons, which certainly drew attention. When the decision was made to discontinue the annual marathon, the club sought new ways to pursue their many goals (particularly that of economic development) and decided the most fruitful effort would be to push for a Mount Baker National Park. Mount Rainier, as mentioned earlier, offered the model. Park designation there in 1899 was proving a definite boost to economic development in communities on the access routes to the park. People were traveling to the new park from all over the United States. Railroads were boosting national parks as great destinations which could be reached (mostly) by rail. Mount Baker National Park promoters had visions of their park as a national destination with all the prosperity that such tourism would bring.

The idea for such a park, but for preservation rather than economic development reasons, had come up around the campfires of the first Mazama outing to the mountain in 1906. During their 1909 outing to the mountain the club acted on the idea by drafting a resolution:

> Resolved by the Mazamas, at a meeting called by the president of the Club at Camp Gorman, on Mount Baker, on the evening of August 7, 1909, that a petition be presented to the Hon. Secretary of the Interior respectfully requesting that Mount Baker, Mount Shuksan and their immediate environs . . . be set aside, dedicated and forever preserved inviolate by the Government of the United States as a park for all the people to be called "The Mount Baker National Park."[1]

The resolution went on to suggest that "merchantable timber" on the public lands in the area be harvested and the proceeds used to construct a road and other improvements on the Middle Fork of the Nooksack. The resolution, though not very specific as to what area the proposed park should encompass, was duly forwarded to the Secretary of the Interior. A copy was sent to the Secretary of Agriculture, under whose jurisdiction the Forest Service managed the land that would be included in the park.

Another resolution to establish a park in the Mount Baker region was introduced in the Washington State Legislature in 1909. The area recommended for inclusion was comprised of eight townships in the northwestern corner of the Washington National Forest, covering the entire Mount Baker Mining District, Hannegan Pass, and the North Fork of the Nooksack and all of its tributaries. This resolution, not surprisingly, stirred up strong opposition among miners struggling to establish lucrative operations in the region. Among others things, they feared that a park would interfere with their plans to build roads through some of the most scenic areas to get their minerals to market.

These resolutions also stirred some response from bureaucrats and politicians in Washington, D.C. In March of 1910 the district forester wrote to the chief forester that he thought the national park idea was a poor one. It would, he thought, curtail development and timber sales. "The existence of the National Forest sufficiently protects the area, while leaving its resources available for development."[2] Despite the district forester's views, the Forest Service considered the idea for three years, even to the point of proposing specific boundaries. Headed by Gifford Pinchot and then by Henry Graves, the Forest Service was philosophically opposed to national parks in general and were fighting against them at that time on other fronts in Montana and Colorado. The core philosophy guiding the Forest Service was that public

Detailed 1912 Mount Baker map, as drawn by C.F. Easton.

lands should be managed for many purposes under a program of balanced use. Parks involved preservation of scenery, which often precluded other uses like logging and mining. Further, parks were administered by the Department of the Interior, and Gifford Pinchot had worked for years to have forest reserves transferred from Interior to the Department of Agriculture. Since he had accomplished this in 1905, his agency and the Department had resisted transfer of any land back to Interior, as would happen when a national park was established by Congress. At the point Mount Baker National Park resolutions were circulating, the National Park Service was still only an idea, and the Forest Service entertained hopes that ultimately it would become keeper of the parks. The major national parks, such as Yellowstone and Yosemite, were being cared for by the U.S. Army.

Despite their resistance to the park idea, the Forest Service apparently thought that Mount Baker would inevitably become a national park, so they sought to minimize the impact of such a park on their jurisdiction by proposing a park of limited extent. Their belief in the probability of park status for the mountain is revealed in the following Forest Service memorandum:

> It is believed that the present conditions surrounding the existing Rainier and Crater Lake National Parks and the territory in the vicinity of Mt. Hood, Mt. Olympus, and Mt. Baker, which are probable locations for future National Parks, require that special attention be given to this matter by the Supervisors of the Forests in the vicinity. Not only should the territory close to the National Parks or probable National Parks be conservatively administered, but lands adjacent to all ways of ingress and egress should also be preserved as nearly as possible in their natural condition.[3]

In June of 1913 the Washington National Forest supervisor presented his park proposal to his superiors. It included approximately fifty thousand acres of "wild, massive, uninhabited, high mountainous country."[4] Most forested areas around the mountain with their merchantable timber were excluded. The Forest Service was ready for the congressional Mount Baker National Park initiative it felt certain was coming.

Charles Finley Easton, now appointed Historian of the Mount Baker Club, began his national park initiative in 1915. He had been privately nurturing the idea since 1903, when he began studying and climbing the mountain. He had been in on Mazama discussions; he knew of the Forest Service proposal and considered it too limited. In his opinion, the Forest Service had too few resources and too little interest to be entrusted with the region as a recreational and scenic resource. A national park administered by the

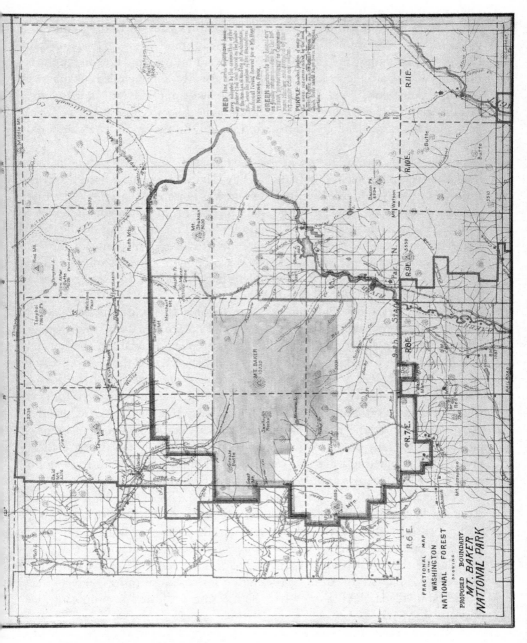

Map of first Mount Baker National Park proposal.

Department of the Interior would ensure better development of the area.

The annual banquet of the Twentieth Century Club in Bellingham provided him with a forum. The Honorable Lin H. Hadley, congressman from the district including the proposed park, would be present. Easton, the featured speaker, both presented the national park idea and unveiled his massive Mount Baker Book, a scrapbook in which he had compiled, during his tenure as Historian of the Mount Baker Club, all the historic, scientific, botanic, geologic and miscellaneous information about the mountain that he could find.

"The leaven began to work," as Easton said later.[5] An outing to the mountain was organized, following Skyline Divide on the new Forest Service trail. Congressman Hadley went along and was honored when the 7,515-foot peak prominent on Chowder Ridge was named for him. The name "Chowder Ridge" also came out of this trip. The group found marine fossils on the ridge that were so complete that Easton made mock chowder of them for dinner. Hadley was most impressed and became a proponent of the park idea. The local press was enthusiastic; Easton noted that "It had the approval of everybody, everywhere."[6]

The Mount Baker Club appointed a National Park Committee to work out a detailed proposal. In the fall of 1915 this committee and Congressman Hadley arranged a meeting in Tacoma with Stephen T. Mather, the Special Assistant to the Secretary of the Interior and soon to be the first Director of the National Park Service, still a year from its creation. Mather, Horace Albright (Mather's young assistant who would one day succeed him as Director of the National Park Service), and other Interior Department officials were touring the nation inspecting parks, promoting creation of new ones, and generally trying to raise public interest in national parks. Others present at the meeting were two veterans of Mount Baker adventures – John A. Lee of the Mazamas and Asahel Curtis of The Mountaineers.

The federal officials expressed enthusiasm about the Mount Baker National Park proposal (though Mather was later to express disinterest in it – there was already a northwest national park featuring a volcano). The only disagreement at the meeting was whether Mount Shuksan should be included. Mather thought it should be in the park. The Mount Baker Club committee had excluded it "out of consideration for certain mining interests that would be involved."[7] All parties left the meeting dedicated to proposing the best possible park.

When all issues of boundary location were resolved between the committee and the Interior Department, Congressman Hadley prepared and introduced in the House of Representatives "A Bill to Establish the Mount Baker National Park in the State of Washington." On January 22, 1916, an identical

Camp Shuksan, 1930s.

bill was introduced in the Senate by Senators Jones and Poindexter. Charles Finley Easton took his huge scrapbook to Washington to lobby for the bill. Hearings were held and reports filed by the Departments of Agriculture and Interior. The former was not happy with the size of the proposed park, for it included merchantable timber. The Department of the Interior was solidly behind the proposed park. The political climate for a new park seemed favorable. A bill to establish the National Park Service was on the congressional docket, and promotion of the national park idea by Mather, Albright, and others was bearing fruit. Proposals for what would become Acadia National Park in Maine, Hawaii National Park, and Lassen Volcanic National Park in northern California were moving toward Congressional approval. Rocky Mountain National Park in Colorado and Glacier National Park in Montana had been established in 1910 and 1915. In all but the Maine and Hawaii cases, national parks had been carved out of national forests. The Forest Service had been opposed, but park promoters had prevailed. The dynamics of Mount Baker National Park politics seemed similar to these earlier successes and gave boosters reason for optimism.

But Mount Baker National Park was not to be. The full docket of park proposals may have been part of the problem. With a northwest volcano already the centerpiece of a park in Mount Rainier, and the eruption of Mount Lassen on May 22, 1915, Mount Baker fell back in the priority list of new parks. Stephen Mather was on a roll but knew he could not argue for all the proposals coming forth. Lassen was already a national monument proclaimed by Theodore Roosevelt, and the eruption made it an especially exciting addition to the national parks. Mount Baker, just another dormant volcano, was pushed back in the queue. The world was at war and the United States was staying out of it in 1916. Domestic matters like parks and park management agencies could be tended to, but when in 1917 the United States declared war on the German Empire, all attention was focused on mobilization for the war effort. Legislation of lesser importance, like the Mount Baker National Park bill, died of neglect. The goal of a national park in the North Cascades with Mount Baker part of it, though pushed to the back burner, would reappear in years to come.

The impetus for development was much diminished while America was involved in the war. After the war, however, development once again became a priority, especially roads and hotel accommodations. When its Mount Baker Park dream failed to reach fruition, the Mount Baker Club quietly faded from influence. A few dedicated members kept the club alive, and it eventually evolved into an outing club that remains active in the 21st century, but its days as a promoter of development were ended.

Charles Finley Easton, ever the Mount Baker enthusiast and booster, continued pursuing his dreams regardless of setbacks and defection of fellow club members. In 1921 he addressed the Bellingham Chamber of Commerce and suggested a new direction for development of the Mount Baker region.

> Mt. Baker was here when man came; it has been here ever since –
> yet even today it is accessible only to persons who have the stamina
> to tread its difficult trails. . .
>
> The construction of what will ultimately be a fine automobile
> road into the Mt. Baker region is the first practical step toward
> enlisting the financial co-operation of visitors in developing the
> region. When such a road is completed, there will be a definite
> objective to automobile tourists. . . . It will make a new era in the
> exploitation of Northwest Washington's scenic attractions, which
> potentially are worth millions and which cannot be excelled any-
> where in the world.[8]

Easton suggested that the best route for the road would be up the North Fork beyond Glacier to Austin Pass. Before the year ended, construction had begun on an eight-foot right-of-way from Excelsior, seven miles beyond Glacier, to the Shuksan townsite, where the road would turn uphill if it were to reach Austin Pass. The key to approval of the project was the willingness of the Forest Service to contribute funds for the road (two federal to each local dollar) which they agreed to do if local national park promoters would cease pushing for a park. Since development was the reason why many park proponents such as the Mount Baker Club had supported a park to begin with, they readily agreed to this deal. If the Forest Service would assist with the developing, that was fine with them. The element of park promoters who saw the park as a means to protect a national treasure *from* development, such as the Mazamas, had moved on to other issues. The Mountaineers, for instance, fought during the 1920s against a proposal favored by the National Park Service to build a round-the-mountain road within Mount Rainier National Park. So, for a time at least, the Forest Service prevailed in its effort to retain administration of lands in the Mount Baker region.

The Forest Service was happy to assist with developing the area. By the 1920s the automobile was becoming more common and use of national forests for recreation was increasing. Initially the Forest Service had supported some recreational use of the lands it administered, as indicated by its willingness to assist the Mazamas in 1906, but promoting or assisting recreation was low on its priority list of tasks. When people began to increasingly use national forests for recreation, and a competitor appeared in the National Park Service (the creation of which had been steadfastly opposed by the Forest Service), the Forest Service attitude changed, and its attention to forest recreation increased. This change was tapped into by Easton and others who refused to give up on their dream of Mount Baker as a tourist destination of national significance.[9]

Road building progressed and a plan emerged to construct a major hotel near Austin Pass. Local supporters included C.H. Park, supervisor of the National Forest; J.P. McMillan, a county commissioner; Bert Huntoon, the engineer who had concluded earlier that a road across the North Cascades was not feasible; and Frank Sefrit, managing editor of the Bellingham newspaper. They attracted financiers and formed a corporation, which they called the Mount Baker Development Company. By early 1923 they had signed a lease for a hotel site in Austin Pass Meadows (known today as Heather Meadows). That summer, using tents, they began their first tourist concession. On a guarantee, backed by a considerable sum of money, that a resort to accommodate tourists would be built on the leased site, the Federal Government agreed to provide funds for construction of a nine-mile road up the hill from Shuksan to the hotel. The federal government, through its agent the Forest Service, would be a partner in this development.

Site work in Austin Pass Meadows began in 1924. A dining hall and bunk house, known as the Heather Inn, were built, along with a stone caretaker's cabin. At Shuksan several cabins and an inn to accommodate fifty people were built. Modern, automobile-based tourism had finally come to the Mount Baker country. Plans for the hotel were presented in 1925, and construction began. The road to the Meadows, renamed Heather Meadows to eliminate confusion with Austin Pass, far above the construction site, was completed in 1926. The name of the national forest itself was changed from Washington National Forest to Mount Baker National Forest. The former name was misleading (people "back east" often thought it included more of the state than it did), and hotel promoters argued that the new name would be very helpful in their advertising and publicity efforts. The Forest Service and the development company built trails to serve hotel clientele. Foresters built a trail around Table Mountain in 1925.

Opening on July 14, 1927, the hotel, called the Mount Baker Lodge, was large and lavish. It was an L-shaped building two hundred and ten feet long and from fifty to one hundred and thirty feet wide with one hundred rooms and a huge dining hall that could seat three hundred. An observation tower rose seventy feet at one end; as many as fifty people could stand at the top and gaze around at the spectacular scenery. Including Heather Inn and thirteen cabins, the resort complex could accommodate three hundred guests and the staff to serve them. The development had its own hydroelectric power system and a fleet of buses to carry guests to and from Bellingham. Many dreams were realized on that July evening when a full lodge enjoyed ceremony, banquet, and dancing.

Charles Finley Easton, getting along in years, does not appear to have been involved in the building of the hotel complex. Still, he must have been satisfied that others had taken his vision seriously. The heavily promoted Mount Baker Lodge was busy throughout the summer of 1927.[10] The Forest Service estimated that 11,700 guests visited the lodge that year for the scenery and social life. Saddle ponies carried guests around Table Mountain. Hikers walked the various trails. Guides were available for climbs of Mounts Shuksan and Baker. Evening entertainment included dancing, movies, and songfests. The lodge became a fashionable place for the affluent to visit and vacation.

The Mount Baker Highway and Lodge allowed thousands of people previously denied a visit to the high country an opportunity to gaze at the glacier-hung bastions of Mount Shuksan, to wander in the alpine meadows, to walk the midsummer snows of the high Cascades. But all of this tourism certainly brought changes to the place. No longer was it the quiet alpine scene it had been when only mountaineers visited Austin Pass. A member of the Mazama outing to the area in 1929 recorded some of the changes.

How strange it must have seemed to the Mount Baker veterans! A splendid inn stands there in the meadows where they had camped

Mount Baker Lodge.

in such solitude ten years before. Roads wind through the shallow glacial valley with cabins popping out on every bend. A mile beyond the inn, in the very eye of the pass, cars were parked that day by the scores; the air reeked with their fumes. On yonder sidehill a searing slash marked the creeping advance of human occupation of this wilderness as a noisy power shovel clattered about its business of taking the road across the pass to the shoulder of Table Mountain. Powdermen with their drills rumbled away on the rocks that ten years ago had housed the marmots. Not so long before the mountain goat had trod that bluff. Air compressors droned their song of demolition.[11]

Mountaineers may have mourned their loss, but for everyone else the changes were good. In the 1920s the lodge and road were the only modern intrusions into thousands of acres of high wilderness country.

Miniature golf at Mount Baker Lodge.

While all the maneuvering for a park and development of roads and lodges were going forward, mountaineering parties continued to visit the mountains. The Mountaineers were back in force in 1916. They came fifty strong on the train from Bellingham to Glacier, then proceeded on foot the fourteen miles to the abandoned town of Shuksan, near the mouth of Swamp Creek, on the North Fork of the Nooksack. The town had sprung up during the gold rush triggered by the Lone Jack strike but had faded quickly as the limits of gold to be found in the area were quickly evident. A six-mile hike up Swamp Creek, along the old miners trail, brought them to Twin Lakes where two thousand gold seekers had once pitched their tents. By 1916 the lakes were entirely abandoned. The Mountaineers climbed Winchester Mountain to survey the countryside then visited the nearby Lone Jack Mine, which was still being worked. From the lakes they set out cross-country for Hannegan Pass at the head of Ruth Creek.

This seems an odd choice of a route to Hannegan Pass, which could have been approached directly up Ruth Creek. But these were mountaineers, and perhaps they wanted to go the way they did for the climbing it would force upon them. They traversed over the shoulder of Goat Mountain and were forced into precarious down-climbing to reach the creek. Eventually they reached their destination where they found "climbing and fishing and vis-

Visitors at Mount Baker Lodge.

iting for three happy care-free days."[12] They climbed Ruth Mountain, and ambitious members of the group toyed with the idea of dropping down to the Nooksack River and making an attempt on Mount Shuksan's imposing northern wall. Instead they hiked down Ruth Creek back to the Shuksan townsite and hiked up to Austin Pass. This would be their base camp for the "big climbs" of Mounts Baker and Shuksan.

Both climbs were successful. Montelius Price, who had made the first ascent with Asahel Curtis, led the three-day Mount Shuksan climb over the route the two had pioneered ten years earlier; twenty five made the ascent. Meanwhile, Curtis led a reconnaissance of Mount Baker. When the Shuksan party returned, thirty aspirants set out for Baker, led by Curtis. They hiked out Ptarmigan Ridge past Coleman Pinnacle, then onto the glaciers for a long

Mount Baker Highway in its early days.

traverse to the cleaver between Boulder and Park glaciers. The line of climbers went up the cleaver and threaded their way upward between many large crevasses onto the summit. The view was clear, the descent uneventful; three weeks after they had started, fifty tired but satisfied Mountaineers emerged from the forest at Concrete on the Skagit River. From Austin Pass they had descended to Swift Creek, then to Baker Lake and Baker River.

At Baker Lake the Mountaineers passed the salmon hatchery built by the state of Washington in 1896. All supplies to build and operate the hatchery had been packed in by mule train from Concrete. The complex consisted of a main hatchery building, barn, tool warehouse, mess hall, twelve-room bunkhouse, and foreman's residence. The main building was new, the original having burned to the ground in 1914. The only large run of sockeye salmon

Mount Baker Lodge, ringed by peaks.

in the Skagit River ran into Baker Lake and the state, responding to a general decline in salmon in Puget Sound, sought to enhance the natural Baker Lake sockeye with hatchery fish. The hatchery complex was a small scar on the wilderness and salmon enhancement the first intensive government resource management effort in the area, but it was a harbinger of things to come to the Mount Baker region.

Other parties, large and small, climbed Mount Baker during this period. The Normal School in Bellingham (later Western Washington University) started its tradition of summer outings to the mountain. The Mazamas returned in 1920, intending to climb the northeastern side, the route that had eluded so many on the first Mazama outing to the mountain in 1906. In 1920 the road ended at Excelsior, so the group of sixty made a fourteen-mile hike from there to Austin Pass, traveling up from Shuksan townsite over a trail recently built by the Forest Service.

Once again John Lee was a climbing leader. While a scouting party examined Mount Shuksan, he led a similar reconnaissance to the top of Mount Baker. Lee's group found the traveling possible but the route finding complex and did not reach the summit until late afternoon. They spent an unplanned night in a crevasse above Boulder-Park Glacier, as Lee had on the first Mazama outing to the area, but suffered no ill effects. Both scouting groups returned to camp. Mount Shuksan was attempted first, and twenty made the summit. Then forty-one Mazamas and five miners who had joined them tackled Mount Baker; they, too, all reached the top. The outing was a resounding success. Not a drop of rain fell on them during the two-week trip, and all of their goals were achieved except repeating the climb that Curtis, Kiser and their four companions had made on the upper Park Glacier in 1906. As climbing leader, Lee opted for a route that many members of the party could manage, for crevasses and steepness made the upper Park Glacier a doubtful path to the summit. Once again the Mazamas thoroughly enjoyed their idyllic campsite in Heather Meadows, innocent of the changes to come.[13]

One change by the time of this outing was that Joe Morovits was no longer in his Baker Lake haunts. Perhaps he tired of his solitary life. He had said he would "stay until I could clean up a few hundred thousand dollars."[14] Maybe he finally admitted to himself that the chances of achieving that goal were slight. Whatever his reasons, after twenty-seven years of exploration and labor in the country east of the mountains, he disappeared, but not unexpectedly. He had sold his mining claims on Sulphide Creek in 1916 to the Mount Shuksan Molybdenite Mine and Milling Company, which was operated by a group from Seattle. In 1917 he sold his homestead and Fourth of July Mines to a group called the Mount Baker Land and Mine Company, one member of which already held a lien on Joe's stamp mill. The company never worked the mines but used the ranch as a hunting and logging camp.

Joe drifted back to coal mining, where he reportedly earned a princely wage of twenty-five dollars a day as a powder monkey. An accident ended this brief lucrative phase of his career when he was struck by a chunk of coal and crippled. The joyful mountain man was forced to wear a neck brace, and his health declined. No one knew for sure, but his friends in Concrete – Baker City when Joe first knew the village – believed that he died alone in some city hospital or nursing home, a sad end for the "hermit of Baker Lake" and Mount Baker's first climbing guide. Yet "he lives, in a way, on his Mount Baker in a hundred stories of derring-do, a kind of Paul Bunyan of the Cascades – Morovits the mighty man."[15]

Others came along to replace him, at least as guides. Visitors to Mount Baker Lodge could hire someone to lead them up either Mount Baker or

Mount Shuksan. Head guide was Bill Cochran, a former coal miner turned YMCA Physical Director and enthusiastic and capable climber. Bill would climb Baker, his favorite mountain, at the slightest provocation. He claimed thirty-nine ascents of the peak between 1912 and 1932. In 1960 Cochran, nearly eighty years old, heard that several men claimed to have made the first complete ascent of Cockscomb Ridge and disputed the claim. He and two companions had climbed it in 1929. He also claimed the first winter ascent of Mount Baker on January 4, 1929.[16]

Among Cochran's fellow guides at the lodge was Ben Thompson, a husky, flamboyant, "Clark Gable type" who specialized in Mount Shuksan climbs. Before he left the area in search of greater fame and fortune as a writer, cartoonist, skier and entrepreneur, he made his mark climbing some new routes on Mount Shuksan. Thompson was also among the first to ski in the Heather Meadows area. The trip in winter up the long, unplowed road from Glacier was long but Thompson and his friends made the trek, opening up the potential of new sport in the area.

The guide who enjoyed the longest career in hobnailed boots and skis was Clarence "Happy" Fisher, a small wiry mountain enthusiast who taught school when he was not climbing. (His teaching career nearly ended when he refused for many years to attend summer school because he was too busy climbing.) He left his name on the region. "Hap" and his buddies thought there must be a shorter route up Mount Shuksan than the long and laborious Curtis Falls route pioneered by Asahel Curtis and Montelius Price on their first ascent. Fisher and Dr. E.P Spearin, a Bellingham dentist, discovered the gully system on the south flank of the mountain known today as the Fisher Chimneys. They climbed Mount Shuksan by that route in 1927. Fisher was first on the summit of several peaks in the area, among them Colfax, the 9,443-foot satellite summit of Mount Baker. He climbed for decades, became the dean of local mountaineers, and was called upon whenever leadership or rescue was required.

These men and a few others led climbs for pay and for fun, in the irrepressible tradition of Joe Morovits. They were local men who loved the local mountains, grabbing any opportunity to go to the high country. No record exists of the extent of their mountain guide business. Few visitors to the lodge aspired to closer views of the big mountains than those from Austin Pass (with its dramatic view of Shuksan) or Artist Point (called Huntoon Point later after the manager of the lodge). But if they wanted to climb, Fisher and his colleagues were ready to show them the way.

The hotel complex was not the only construction close to the mountain during this era. The Mount Baker Club did some building of its own. Before the 1912 marathon they had constructed a "shelter cabin" at Mazama Park on

Ben Thompson

Shelter cabin at Mazama Park.

Ridley Creek, at the head of the Middle Fork of the Nooksack River. This cabin served racers and officials on the Middle Fork race course. The club also hoped to build another cabin somewhere along the Glacier Trail route. In 1912 Henry Engberg and Charles Finley Easton scouted for a site and fixed on Heliotrope Ridge, elevation approximately five thousand feet. Their vision at the time was of a stone structure with six sleeping rooms, a large living room, a double fireplace and a porch all around. Coleman Glacier was nearby.

The club began raising money for the project, but the financial burden of staging the marathon was more than it had anticipated. A modest shelter was built on the site Engberg and Easton had selected. After the races were cancelled, the club took a few years to retire race-related debts. When the First World War interfered with its national park hopes, the club almost died but a few people remained active, including Easton, and in the early 1920s it began to revive. Fund-raising for a cabin was renewed, and support for the project grew. Finally in October of 1925, Kulshan Cabin was dedicated on a tributary of Grouse Creek, ten miles up the trail from Glacier, just below timberline a short distance west of Heliotrope Ridge. The log structure could shelter a substantial party and provide the club and others with a base for climbing and hiking on the mountain.

The effort of constructing the cabin seems to have once again sapped the strength and finances of the Mount Baker Club, which was forced to reorganize and incorporate again in June of 1928. With the old roster of eighty members forming its nucleus, the new corporation assumed the debts of the old club. This new Mount Baker Club, while retaining the long-standing goals of drawing public attention to the scenic beauties of the region and encouraging development and study, declared itself an outing club. Its primary goal would be to engage in mountaineering in the North Cascade Mountains. Among its leaders were Will Pratt of the original 1911 group and young climbers and skiers like Hap Fisher and Dr. Spearin. They got things moving, and in 1929 the club scheduled nineteen outings, published a newsletter and carried on the tradition begun nearly twenty years earlier of helping people enjoy the scenic beauties of the Mount Baker area.

The building of the Mount Baker Highway and the lodge at Heather Meadows was certainly a dream come true for many, particularly for engineer Bert Huntoon and visionary Charles Finley Easton. The resort development, with its roads, guides, and skiers changed the region more abruptly and finally than any human agents had before. Climbers continued to flock to Mount Baker, but the pioneering shifted to the rocks and glaciers of Mount Shuksan and other North Cascade peaks.

The first Kulshan Cabin, 1925.

Joe Morovits' departure marked the end of an era. Opportunity had been limited in the region for independent, solitary, hardy souls like Joe, but a few had tried with modest means and remarkable perseverance to make their lives in this demanding landscape. Joe had failed to get rich but seems to have prospered in other ways. Eventually he moved on, with little more to show for his labors than memories of great virgin forests and high mountain scenery. And he was the last; there are no more mysterious and romantic characters of his stature in the Mount Baker story.

9

Hard Times and Skiers: 1930-1950

Be it enacted ... that for the purpose of relieving the acute conditions of wide-spread distress and unemployment now existing in the United States, and in order to provide for the restoration of the country's depleted resources ... the President is authorized ... to provide for employing citizens of the United States who are unemployed, in the construction, maintenance and carrying on of works of a public nature in connection with the forestation of lands belonging to the United States. ...

– The Emergency Conservation Work Act,
March 31, 1933

Early in the morning of August 3, 1931, Bert Huntoon was out in the meadows near Mount Baker Lodge taking pictures of the sunrise. The morning was beautiful. There was little wind. The first rays of the sun would soon strike the high summits to the north. All was still except for a distant roar of water and the pipings of juncos and chickadees. Suddenly Huntoon's reverie was destroyed by the fire alarm at the lodge. Rushing across the heather, he was shocked to see flames already racing across the roof. Men were shouting and running and struggling with hose lines. Even as he ran for the building it seemed hopeless – the fire had a fast start.

Huntoon and other hotel staff rushed through the burning building yelling and kicking at doors to make sure all guests made their way to safety. The walls of the lobby, dining room, and corridors were covered with cedar shakes, which burned furiously. A tank containing nineteen hundred gallons of fuel oil exploded. Soon the building was an inferno as flames leaped hundreds of feet into the air, their roar – almost a shriek – likened by spectators to the sound of a steam whistle. The fire crew with its seven hoses could but

Ruins of Mount Baker Lodge, 1931.

stand by and watch, and in two hours the magnificent lodge was a smoking ruin.

The Mount Baker Lodge had lasted only five years, but its impact had been great. Thousands of people had discovered the delights of Heather Meadows, Mount Shuksan and Mount Baker. A good road had been built – ironically, at the time of the fire the highway department was nearing completion of the highway extension three miles beyond Heather Meadows to Artist Point. The thirty-two-room annex, all the guest cabins and the Heather Inn survived the blaze and could still accommodate one hundred guests. People continued to come, but the dazzle and glory of the beautiful hotel was gone. The Development Company, which was really just getting started, could ill afford such a loss, particularly since its insurance only partially covered its quarter-million dollar investment in the resort. On top of this, the nation was in the throes of a deep depression. Few People had the means to visit such a place. The wealthy would have come to the lodge despite the depression, but without the hotel the resort could not offer the glamour and luxury sought by such people. The company never recovered from the fire.

The development company may have fallen on hard times, but the recently reorganized Mount Baker Club was going strong. Its members were traveling all over Mount Baker country, led by Hap Fisher and other veterans of its meadows and crags. Skiing was becoming increasingly popular with club members. Parties were vying for the first ski ascent of Mount Baker and several attempts were made during the winter of 1930-31. The Mount Baker Ski Club acquired a cabin, known as Verona Cabin, four miles up the highway from Shuksan on a mining claim. Beginning in 1931, regular winter outings were made for skiing in the Heather Meadows area. Ten such trips were made that winter.

Skiing near Mount Baker Lodge, late 1920s.

These winter trips were quite an undertaking. Skiers could drive to Glacier and as far beyond as road conditions would allow. In the early 1930s the Highway Department made no effort to keep the road open beyond Excelsior, seven miles east of Glacier. When the snow line was low, visitors had to hike or ski another 6.7 miles from there to Shuksan, or 11.7 miles to Verona Cabin. Skiers then had to climb with their long wooden skis yet another four miles beyond the cabin to Heather Meadows. Then, if they wanted any downhill runs, they had to "bust the powder" or pack the snow by side-stepping (which is very difficult in the huge snowfalls for which Heather Meadows is famous). Mount Baker skiing at this time was a sport only for the strong and dedicated. From the beginning skiing in Heather Meadows was referred to as "skiing Mount Baker." This is a misnomer still applied today to a day of skiing in the Mount Baker Ski Area. The mountain lording it over the area to the east is Mount Shuksan, which is much closer than Baker seven miles to the south and invisible from most of the ski runs.

The approach to Heather Meadows continued to be strenuous for skiers through the winter of 1933. In January of that year the Development Company's caretaker at its Shuksan Inn cleared a quarter-mile ski runway there, nine miles below Heather Meadows on the highway. Forty to fifty

A Mountaineers cabin in 2010.

Spring skiing near Mount Baker Lodge, late 1920s.

skiers came to enjoy it. Snow at Shuksan was three and a half feet deep; the Highway Department was prevailed upon to keep the road open as far as the inn. But heavy snow later in the month defeated the plow crew's somewhat half-hearted efforts (their equipment was sadly inadequate), and once again it was quite a trek to reach good skiing. Still, despite the slog to get there, more skiers made their way up to Heather Meadows.

The property on which the Verona Cabin stood was sold to a mining company in December of 1934, and while the new owners assured the Mount Baker Club skiers that they could continue to use their cabin, the group decided that such an arrangement was too uncertain to suit them. They formally organized the Mount Baker Ski Club (still affiliated at this point with the Mount Baker Club) and set out to build their own cabin. They designed a forty-by-twenty-foot structure that would sleep up to sixty-five skiers. By December of 1935 it was completed at Camp Four, just below Heather Meadows, on Galena Creek.

By this time the road was finally being kept open to the meadows in winter. In 1934 a Hollywood film company decided that the area was ideal for the filming of "The Call of the Wild," Jack London's story of the far north, starring Clark Gable and Loretta Young. A Klondike village appeared in Heather Meadows in January of 1935, and more than a hundred people worked there on the film.[1] Highway crews, using a new rotary plow, struggled with a series of blizzards to keep the road open, failing at times. When the last of the cameramen left in mid-February, the Highway Department decided to plow the road to Heather Meadows for the rest of the winter. Skiers rejoiced and enjoyed the first full winter of snow sports there. The highway was cleared throughout the winter for the remainder of the 1930s, until World War II made gasoline too expensive to run the plows.

Skiing grew in popularity, drawing increasing winter visitation to Heather Meadows. In May 1935, the Pacific Northwest Ski Association held its first slalom meet at Panorama Dome above Heather Meadows. One hundred and thirty skiers raced and several thousand spectators watched them. So many skiers ventured to the area that an enterprising logger named Arthur Brandlund designed an "escalator" to transport them up Panorama Dome. This was a hoisting sled that could carry up to twenty skiers from an elevation of 4,200 feet to 5,100 feet in less than five minutes. The sled was pulled up the steep slope on a steel cable by a double-drum donkey engine concealed in the trees at the top of the slope. The Forest Service allowed the operator to charge a small fee, which was not to exceed twenty-five cents a trip. Skiers were willing to pay this exorbitant price (high for the time); the climb up the face was long, steep, and exhausting in the unpacked snow. This ingenious contraption had been operating only a month when, early in January of 1936, an avalanche hit Brandlund and two companions as they made their way up the haul-back cable to start the day's operation. Brandlund was killed and the experiment ended. With the demise of the "escalator," the Development Company decided to try a more conventional lift and installed a rope tow.

Five hundred skiers schussed the slopes above Heather Meadows throughout the winter of 1936, and in May as many as a thousand visited the area on a good weekend in hundreds of cars. Promoters waxed eloquent about the potential of this new sport, but they knew that the resort must be improved if growth were to continue. A bigger and better hotel – a replacement for the Mount Baker Lodge – was essential. The nation was slowly pulling itself out of the Great Depression, and in 1937 the directors of the Mount Baker Development Company began working with the Forest Service on plans for a new $1.5 million hotel on the site of the ill-fated lodge. The hope was that the Federal Government, through its Works Progress Administration, would build the facility. Despite much hoping and scheming, nothing came of the idea.

The Mount Baker region saw other developments in the 1930s unrelated to skiing. The Civilian Conservation Corps (CCC) worked on many projects. The CCC was established in 1933 as a New Deal program of the Franklin

CCC crew constructing forest-camp table and benches at Baker Lake, 1936.

Roosevelt administration to put unemployed young men to work, help them learn useful skills, and do necessary conservation work throughout the United States. Men were organized into camps administered by the US Army and worked on public lands with the cooperation and supervision of federal resource-management agencies like the Forest Service and Park Service. Two camps were sited in the vicinity of Mount Baker, one in the Glacier Ranger District and one in the Baker River District; both worked on Forest Service projects.

The Glacier District camp was established in 1933, first on the banks of the Nooksack River near the village of Shuksan, then on Boulder Creek five miles west of Glacier.[2] Camp Glacier, as it was called, consisted initially of five Army officers and enlisted men and two hundred CCC men, of whom forty-five were "Local Experienced Men" (LEMs). Many LEMs were skilled woodsmen and supervised and instructed groups of "enrollees," younger men who, though physically able, lacked experience in use of tools and skills necessary to do the work. Enrollees came from all over America; many in Camp Glacier came from the Midwest.

CCC recruits would start as laborers and with experience graduate to

Forest fire training at the Glacier CCC camp, 1933.

one of the more specialized crews. Activities were divided into several major areas: timber improvement, soil conservation, construction, and fire prevention and suppression. Jobs included carpentry, vehicle maintenance, saw filing, tree trimming and thinning, and trail construction.

Camp Glacier men compiled an impressive list of achievements in their seven years in the District, before the Second World War brought the demise of the program. They built a temporary camp near Shuksan, then a more permanent one at Boulder Creek, several miles west of Glacier. They improved and extended the road toward Hannegan Pass and built a road from Shuksan to within two miles of Twin Lakes. They constructed over forty-three miles of surfaced truck roads, including those starting up Wells and Canyon Creeks. They developed four lookouts and eleven campgrounds and expanded the Glacier Ranger Station. A major revegetation effort was launched at Heather Meadows to repair damage caused by too many "social trails" during the heyday of the lodge. And they built a fine structure, the Austin Pass

Warming Hut, above the meadows. Trails were constructed and improved, trees pruned, snags felled, telephone lines installed and repaired. More than one hundred miles of telephone lines eventually connected the Glacier Ranger Station and its fire lookouts. Storms constantly damaged these lines, keeping CCC crews busy.

Housing thirty men, the Baker Lake camp was smaller than Camp Glacier. A road had been pushed up Baker River to Baker Lake in the late 1920s and early 1930s. Permanent district headquarters had been established at Koma Kulshan, below Baker Lake. The U.S. Bureau of Fisheries was still trying to operate its hatchery at the lake, but heavy snow again flattened the main building. The CCC men built a new hatchery and water system, and operation resumed in 1939. CCC crews also worked to complete recreation facilities like campgrounds around Baker Lake.

The CCC left a lasting impression on the Mount Baker region. Their road building opened areas previously accessible only to hikers. Eventually

Forest Service packtrain leaving Glacier.

some of the roads they started would become major long-hauling thorough-fares. Their construction of lookouts and telephone lines enabled the Forest Service to extend its protective eye and more effectively suppress forest fires. Its campground and trail construction provided facilities for growing public interest in outdoor recreation. Thanks to the CCC, the 1930s may well have been the high-water mark of recreation development in the Mount Baker region.

The 1930s saw the installation of fire lookouts in the region from which a fire watch was kept during fire seasons until the last fire guard shuttered the lookout cabin atop Winchester Mountain in 1967. The first fire look-out cabin in the area was built on Church Mountain in 1928. Others were built on Baker Point and Park Butte south of Mount Baker, and on Excelsior Peak, Winchester Mountain, and Goat Mountain to the north. All were built in the 1930s. Fire guards were on duty in some of these places even before cabins were built to house them. Guards lived below their peak and hiked daily to their posts. The guard at Winchester Mountain, for example, camped for several seasons at Twin Lakes before the CCC built a cabin on the peak.

These fire guards had lonely and rugged duty. They would generally arrive at their posts in late June and depart in late August, though this might vary with weather conditions. Sometimes they arrived before the snow was out; the trail to Winchester Mountain was regularly blocked by snow until the middle of July. When this was the case, the lookout had to trudge up and down the mountain, transporting supplies in small amounts on his or her back until the packer and his horses could get through. Marian Enyeart, a lookout on Winchester Mountain in the 1950s, described her 12-by-12 foot home:

> The cabin was furnished with a bunk, stove, table, a few cupboards, a stool with glass insulators on the legs, a washtub, a leaky dishpan, a bucket and some pots, pans and utensils (usually rusty), a mop, and a broom with no handle. There was a Coleman gas lantern, a kerosene lamp, some tools, a shovel and an ax, and a water-can backpack, with a spray pump to use for fire suppression.[3]

Lookout life was quiet most of the time. Occasionally there would be a long spell of dry weather when fire danger would rise to a high level. Sharp and constant attention was required of the guard during such periods. At other times the fog and rain would close in, completely obscuring visibility, sometimes for days or even weeks. Guards would snuggle into the sleeping bag to sleep, read, or pass the time any way they could. The stove did little to chase the damp chill at such times, and fuel was always scarce. Rare lightning storms provided some excitement. The lookout then perched on the insulated stool, spotting and locating every lightning strike. When the storm passed,

Austin Pass Ski Shelter under CCC construction, 1940.

the lookout would continue to watch these strikes and report any smoke to Glacier by telephone if the line had not gone down in the storm as it sometimes did. Lookouts in the Glacier District could communicate with each other and District Headquarters in Glacier through a switchboard at the Silver Fir Guard Station near Shuksan. They called in on a regular schedule, their primary contact with the outside world except for the occasional hiker or packer who visited their scenic perches. A lonely life, but the scenery was grand; many lookouts returned for duty year after year.

As the 1930s drew to a close, recreational use of the Mount Baker region continued to increase. The Mount Baker Development Company continued its operation at Heather Meadows. The road was open all year, and several major ski meets were held. The Forest Service reported that recreation visitors to the Mount Baker National Forest as a whole had been an estimated 27,498 in 1924 with no recorded winter sports. Fifteen yeas later the total was an estimated 132,000; 48,500 of these were winter visitors.[4] Nearly all winter visits were recorded at Heather Meadows. This was significant growth; promoters and developers were hopeful of a prosperous future, but world events once again affected their aspirations and plans.

When the United States entered World War II late in 1941, people sud-

Slalom race, 1930s.

Heather Inn.

denly had far less time and money for outdoor recreation. Gasoline shortages made it impossible for the Highway Department to keep the road to Heather Meadows open. With no income generated the Development Company went bankrupt; its property was sold at a sheriff's sale. During the war the facilities at Heather Meadows, both those in private and Forest Service hands, were virtually abandoned. Occasional parties from the Mount Baker Ski Club still visited the Meadows, but most of the time winter silence returned.

The Forest Service continued it fire surveillance, bolstered in 1942 by an Aircraft Warning Service run by the Army with Forest Service cooperation. Twenty-four observation posts were activated in the Glacier District, and sixty employees were added. This system operated until the winter of 1943, when diminishing threats of a Japanese air attack and heavy snow drove observers from their stations.

Mount Baker Club activities were also curtailed during the war. Many club members went into the service. The ski cabin and Kulshan Cabin fell into disrepair. A few hiking groups ventured into the high country during the summers of the war years, but human activity on and around Mount Baker was the lowest since 1891.

After the war, people came back to the mountains. A new company was formed to revive the ski resort. The buildings at Heather Meadows were repaired and reopened, and in the spring of 1946 the Bagley rope tow was restarted. Climbers returned to the mountains in search of ever more difficult challenges. The Mount Baker Club, now primarily a hiking club, resumed its visits. And the Forest Service dedicated itself increasingly to harvest of the rich timber resources of the Mount Baker region.

No road yet reached up Glacier Creek in 1946, nor did a road reach very far up the Middle Fork of the Nooksack. The country around the mountain remained largely wild and pristine. In the late 1940s the Forest Service, responding to a rapid growth in demand for timber in the post-war period, began pushing roads up these valleys. The Seaboard Logging Company built a road and began cutting timber in the Glacier Creek watershed. As the decade drew to a close, the road reached to within two miles of Kulshan Cabin, which was just below timberline below Coleman Glacier. The cabin had not been maintained during the 1940s and was in bad shape. Consequently, when the Glacier Creek Road opened for public use, the Mount Baker Club and Western Washington State College, who jointly maintained the cabin, decided that a new building was needed. They removed the old one in 1951 and built another close by the original site. Climbers and hikers would still have a destination and shelter high on the slopes of Mount Baker. The cabin was ultimately removed by the Forest Service in the 1980s because it was again in disrepair and by then inside the boundaries of the Mount Baker Wilderness.

The post-war period saw a new breed of mountaineer. These climbers would not be content to simply follow the standard routes up the mountain pioneered earlier in the century by a generation of mountaineers using relatively primitive equipment and technique. Post-war climbers would come to the Pacific Northwest's great peaks with a thirst for bold and difficult ways to the summits. They would find them.

10

Modern Mountaineering

"A man does not climb a mountain without bringing some of it away with
him and leaving something of himself upon it."
— Sir Martin Conway

Edmund Coleman sought the line of least resistance to Mount Baker's
summit. Merely getting up there was challenge enough for him. His dis-
tinction was that he was first. After Coleman, however, simply reaching the
top was not challenge enough for some climbers. They sought new and unexplored ways up the mountain. Over the years they found many ways to climb
its south, east, and northeast slopes. Unclimbed north and northwest walls
looked simply impossible, so ambitious young climbers took them on.

These walls are steep, and while they may not seem daunting in today's
world of advanced equipment and technique, they were a formidable challenge in the "old days." The north face is bordered on the south by a rotten
volcanic ridge called the Roman Nose and on the northeast by the long
Cockscomb Ridge. The face is split by the North Ridge, the upper part of
which is capped by part of Roosevelt Glacier. The entire face is imposing.
Coleman Headwall, lying between the Roman Nose and North Ridge, consists of steep ice and unstable rock. Roosevelt Headwall, on the other side of
the North Ridge, is a steep and heavily crevassed glacier. Eighty years passed
after Coleman's first ascent before anyone climbed this face.

The key figure in the exploration of this side of the mountain was Fred
Beckey. Raised in the Northwest, Beckey was drawn to the mountains at
the age of thirteen. The Boy Scouts and The Mountaineers gave him his
start and basic techniques, and before long Beckey emerged as one of the
outstanding young climbers in America. He first came to Mount Baker in
1939 and followed Joe Morovits' footsteps up Boulder Glacier. In March of
1947 he returned to the mountain and climbed it on skis. The challenge of

Fred Beckey, photo by fellow climber John A. Rupley.

the unclimbed north face beckoned him, but a busy season climbing in the British Columbia Coast Mountains precluded a return until the summer of 1948.

The face was still untouched when Beckey, with cousins Ralph and Dick Widrig, approached the mountain up the newly built logging road that had superseded the Glacier Creek Trail to within two miles of Kulshan Cabin. After a night in the cabin, the three men threaded their way through the crevasses of Coleman Glacier to the base of the North Ridge. The lower part of the ridge required step-kicking; as the slope gradually steepened the trio put on their crampons. They made steady upward progress, slowly approaching the ice cliff that caps the ridge at 9,600 feet, the most difficult part of the climb. In his account of his North Cascades climbing exploits, *Challenge of the North Cascades*, Beckey describes how the difficulties were overcome.

Fatigue had made the ice wall seem impossibly distant, though in fact only a few hundred feet above. Soon we saw that to outflank the worst parts we would have to climb its left edge, where the ridge narrows quite sharply. The wall on the right is shorter but more vertical; the ridge, rising at an angle varying between 50° and 65° looked more feasible.

. . . to the left we stared down the longest ice slopes we had seen that summer, and to the right the wall fell away to a steep cliff of rotten lava and black ice. Where the angle increased above 45° Ralph chopped a large stance in the ice, and when he had his belay ready I began chopping a line up the steep ridge . . . . For two arduous hours I chopped, maintaining a delicate, strained balance on chipped-out handholds. On the second lead, though, we had a bit of luck: a curious small ice cavern large enough for a cold sitting belay. Ralph did all the shivering belaying of those 2 hours; Dick came last, hacking out the pitons as he climbed. Above the wall the slope angle decreased, but hopes for fast, non-belayed progress were premature. The crest became blue ice covered with loose snow and filmy crusts so variable in depth we could not trust ice ax belays. We were forced to excavate large stances for body belays, and to scrape away lose material before cutting a step. But despite all problems the ridge was exhilarating, a celestial pathway with only blue sky above. The covering on the ice became thicker; it was a relief to reach a wall of compact nevé. The interminable slope suddenly eased off and we stood on a nearly level ridge crest with the summit visible only a few hundred feet above. A giant berg-schrund blocked passage directly ahead to the summit dome, so we made a traverse left between large crevasses toward the exact summit, a little pumice mound peeping through the ice. Ten hours had elapsed since we left the cabin.[1]

The wall so many climbers had decided was beyond them had yielded in almost routine fashion. The climb had been straightforward except for the ice cliff; it would become a popular moderate route for modern climbers with their improved tools and technique.

Beckey could see good routes on the glacial headwalls on both sides of the North Ridge and intended to be the first to climb them. Coleman Glacier Headwall was climbed, however, before he could get to it. This headwall rises from about 8,300 feet to 10,500 feet, with over 2000 feet of climbing on slopes averaging forty-five degrees. It consists of a series of short ice cliffs bordered by the Roman Nose on the south and a rock face and ice rim on the northeast. The face is raked at times by falling ice and rock.

On August 18, 1957, Phil Bartow, Ed Cooper, Don Grimlund and Dave Nicholson made the first ascent of this headwall. They approached the climb across the Coleman Glacier and started up an avalanche cone that lay at the foot of the face between two rock islands. They encountered difficulties immediately, for a crevasse blocked their path, forcing them to traverse to the right on hard, steep snow toward the rock island. When they could turn upward again, they had to climb a steep pitch of ice, followed by two hundred feet of moderate climbing.

After this stretch of relatively easy going, the climbing again became difficult. Cooper describes it:

After some 60' of 60° slopes, one man finally reached a belay spot with standing-room only in a crevasse. The knife edge ridge of the lower lip of the crevasse was traversed to a point where the two lips joined, and Bartow surmounted a 5' near vertical section.[2]

This steep step behind them, they worked their way up several hundred feet

Climbers near Sherman Crater on Mount Baker.

of forty-five-to-fifty-degree snow slopes until they found themselves beneath the upper ice cliffs. Moving to the right, they climbed through these obstacles where two large crevasses bisect the upper portion of the face. Several hundred feet of steep climbing along a narrow rock outcropping brought them to the point where the angle of the face eased off to the summit plateau. Almost twelve hours of strenuous climbing enabled them to make the first ascent of Coleman Headwall.

A prize coveted by Beckey had gone to someone else, but just barely. His busy climbing schedule brought him to the mountain for this very climb a few weeks later. Roosevelt Headwall remained to be done, so he put it on his schedule for the following year.

Before Beckey returned, two Canadian climbers found a variation of the Coleman Headwall route. In May, 1958, Henryk Mather and Les MacDonald of Vancouver, B.C., started up the avalanche cone as their predecessors had. Instead of veering to the right, though, they went directly up the face, and in doing so had to negotiate some very dangerous and loose ice rubble. At one point they were blocked by a rock and ice pillar but climbed around it on very steep ice and continued straight up it until they could penetrate the ice cliffs of the summit cap.[3] Mather and MacDonald had found a more direct and dangerous way up the headwall and pushed the challenge of climbing Mount Baker up the scale of difficulty.

Fred Beckey came back in June, this time with Don Gordon and John Rupley. Their objective was the Roosevelt Glacier Headwall. This steep, heavily crevassed and avalanche-prone glacial headwall is bordered on the south by the North Ridge, on the northeast by the Cockscomb Ridge. Beckey, Gordon, and Rupley traversed across the Coleman Glacier and started upward. Threading among the crevasses, they traversed left, or eastward, and up the left side of the glacier. It steepened at about 9,500 feet; they climbed a corridor between crevasses and up moderately steep firn and ice until they reached the lower lip of the great upper bergschrund, which slashes across the entire upper face. Avalanche debris provided a bridge across this huge crevasse. They then climbed the nearly vertical ice of its upper lip using ice pitons for safety. Finally they traversed diagonally leftward until they reached the upper part of Cockscomb Ridge, which they climbed to the summit. Three major features of Mount Baker's north face had been climbed. Its two containing features – Cockscomb Ridge and the Roman Nose – remained to be done. Both yielded to climbers in 1960.

Ed Cooper was back in search of another first ascent in June. Two years before he had climbed the mountain with his eye on the Roman Nose but had been intimidated by the rotten rock. He had climbed a new route on Colfax Peak, the eastern Black Butte that rises across Coleman Glacier from the Nose. He came back to try the Nose again, accompanied by Gordon Thompson, Mike Swayne and Don Ihlenfeldt. The party hiked to the base of the two-thousand-foot snakelike cleaver and found a snow finger that gave access to its crest of mud-lava. "After several discouraging leads," wrote Cooper, "we found that we could traverse on 45-50° snow just below and east of the ridge crest." This was greatly preferable to the rotten rock of the cleaver. They worked upward this way for a thousand feet and came to a vertical step in the ridge. This forced them to the right on a series of ledges, where they encountered black ice and had to chop steps. Surmounting the steep icy section, they continued upward on rotten rock until they reached yet another steep step. "While pitons would have been desirable, they were impossible to fix," noted Cooper."[4] Largely without protection, the four men again traversed to the right, this time in deep, wet snow over black ice. Two hundred feet of this insecure work brought them to a short rock pitch inundated with meltwater; they climbed up the pitch onto the ridge crest. The rock ridge gradually merged with a snow ridge, which they then followed, much relieved to be on relatively firm ground, onto the summit plateau.

Cooper's account of this climb gives the distinct impression that it was an unpleasant and dangerous venture. The party faced and met severe challenges – exciting but far from ideal conditions on the route. The climb was danger-

Panorama of searching party crossing snow bridge on Coleman Glacier, July 1939.

ous throughout because of the poor rock and lack of protection. A winter
ascent of the route was made in January 1977 by Anton Karuza and Greg
Thompson. With the mud-lava solidly frozen, they climbed more directly
and with more security. They were able to climb chimneys and cracks, using
nuts for protection, and avoid the traverses that rotten rock had forced on the
first ascent party. Their climb was challenging and enjoyable, and conditions
were good. Weather was unusually stable for winter, and there was very little
snow. Ordinarily, winter climbing on the mountain is difficult, but the unusually dry winter of 1977 gave Karuza and Thompson a great opportunity and
they took advantage of it.[5]

Cockscomb Ridge, which had frustrated so many aspirants beginning
with Dorr and his partner in 1882, was also finally climbed in 1960.[6] Parties
had come up to the crumbly rock protuberance at 9,500 feet from various
directions – Dorr and others from Skyline Divide and Chowder Ridge;
Morovits, the Mazamas and others from Ptarmigan Ridge and Park Glacier

on the east. They had either been stopped by the obstacle, or bypassed it. No one had taken on the Cockscomb (referred to in early accounts as Pumice-stone Pinnacle) directly and continued up the ridge to the summit. John Musser, Chuck Morley and Klindt Vielbig tackled this touchy challenge on July 4, 1960.

The three approached the problem across Coleman and Roosevelt glaciers from Kulshan Cabin and climbed onto the ridge at the 8,800 foot level. From there they ascended the gradually steepening ridge, encountering tricky crevasses at 9,000 feet. A cliff of crumbly rock dropped steeply down to the Roosevelt Glacier on their right. A steep and crevassed tongue of Mazama Glacier sloped down to the left. Thin snow bridges enabled them to cross the crevasses, but they were then forced to make a long contour to the left, or east, in order to get around the bergschrund at the head of Mazama Glacier. Snow slopes led to mud-lava, and they finally reached the ridge crest and the Cockscomb.

At this point they were benighted and bivouacked just below their major problem. Next morning they tackled the "tower," which "was gained in the most direct line by steep snow on the east side." Climbing the "rock" of the pinnacle itself was utterly impossible for it was extremely crumbly volcanic material. At one time the pinnacle had been a double formation, but one of two pillars had fallen away onto Roosevelt Glacier, testimony to its extreme instability. The three climbers stayed as high as they could in order to claim a direct ascent of the ridge. As they traversed past the three-hundred-foot pinnacle they were on very steep snow, but they made the passage without mishap, regained the crest of the ridge, and continued on to the top. Modern technique and snow and ice-climbing gear allowed a more direct ascent than had been possible for any of the earlier aspirants. Mountaineering had come a long way since Joe Morovits initially probed the area for a route, equipped only with his hobnail boots and rifle. Even so, climbers could still not safely climb "mud-lava" and the party had not been able to climb the Cockscomb as such. They climbed the ridge as directly as it can safely be done.

The major routes on Mount Baker itself had been climbed, but there were other fields in the area for climbers in search of firsts. As noted earlier, Ed Cooper and Fergus O'Conner came to the mountain in early May of 1959 intent on climbing the Roman Nose, only to give up the idea because the good early season conditions they had hoped for were denied them. Instead, they turned their attention to the unclimbed ice wall rising between the lower and main East Peak of Black Butte. The climb is known as the North Face route of Colfax Peak, and Cooper and O'Conner found it steep but surprisingly easy, thanks to unusual conditions. Huge ice blocks had avalanched off the glacier high on the peak, as they regularly do, but these blocks, instead of roaring down on to Coleman Glacier in their normal fashion, had lodged in the bergschrund and formed a bridge. Snow covered the bridge, and the two were able to climb over it and up through the gap left by the falling ice in the overhanging ice cliff. The climbers went up a steep ramp in snow soft enough for "excellent buckets" and had their first ascent.[7]

The other major summit of the Black Buttes, 9,096-foot Lincoln Peak had, two years earlier, proved a more challenging climb. Early in the morning of July 27, 1956, Fred Beckey, Wes Grande, John Rupley, and Herb Staley set out from Kulshan Cabin intent on the first ascent of Lincoln Peak. They climbed Heliotrope Ridge, from which they gazed across the 1,500-foot deep chasm of Thunder Glacier at their objective. They paused a while to ponder the desirable prospect of "basking amid lupine and fireweed for the day."[8] But ambition triumphed over lassitude, and they were soon sliding down to the glacier. They traversed below its snout and then beneath the western face of the butte.

Examining the south face towering above them, the four men found that it "presented a vast forest of lava rock in various stages of decay."[9] Its apron was a steep glacier, above which was a maze of gullies topped by four towers. They climbed the glacier, negotiated the moat above it, and started up the largest gully toward the second tower from the left. As they climbed, the "hollow echo of falling rock above revealed the presence of an anti-social billy goat within 300 feet of our summit choice."[10]

The men abandoned most of their climbing hardware, thinking that if a goat could do the climb they certainly could follow without much technical difficulty. Up the gully they went for a thousand feet on loose snow and rock lying at a steep fifty-five degree angle, and by 1 p.m. they were looking over a col above the north face. From here they turned to the left, or westward, 150 feet below their summit tower. Clouds blanketed the mountain and valleys below, though they could occasionally look through "veiled windows" at climbers on the Coleman Glacier.[11]

The next 150 feet of work required great care, for they climbed over loose blocks, then up a rotten forty-foot chimney that required stemming, and an exposed, narrow crack. Finally reaching the top of their tower, the four gazed in frustration across at the true summit eighty feet higher. Not about to quit short of the top, they rappelled into the forty-foot gap separating the towers, fixed a rope for the return trip and climbed to the summit. "At approximately 3 p.m., well chilled and cheated of a view, we emptied a sardine can as a register and affixed a jaunty red ribbon to the cairn."[12] After a dangerous descent they returned to their camp fifteen hours after leaving it. Herb Staley drolly summed up the adventure: "Basically, the climb is a problem in route-finding, but the attendant hazards more than compensate for any lack of technical dif-

Large crevasse with snow bridges.

ficulty. None of us would care to repeat the climb or to recommend it."[13]

The search for "firsts" on the mountain continues to the present though today people break new ground with skies, snowboards, paragliders, and other new sports, equipment, and approaches to adventure. In 1961 a party climbed Easton Glacier to a notch at 9,600 feet on the Easton-Talum Cleaver. Instead of climbing westward up Baker's main peak as other parties had done (beginning with the 1909 Mazama climb), they descended into the crater. The group explored a bit, examining steam vents and the crater outlet onto Boulder Glacier, then climbed Boulder Glacier northward to the summit.

In 1970 a party forged a new route up Park Glacier Headwall, climbing directly up its middle. The upper part of the climb was steep and difficult, involving negotiation of a *bergschrund* and cornice. A party of five from Oregon climbed a new variation up Roosevelt Glacier the same year. In January of 1977 the first winter ascent of the Roman Nose was completed. In years since, with many advances in climbing equipment, particularly for ice climbing, a multitude of variations on established routes too numerous to describe have been accomplished. One interesting wrinkle on the search for firsts is that people have forced first *descents* as they pointed their skis and snowboards down amazing slopes, off ice cliffs and around crevasses on routes that earlier generations of skiers and climbers could not have imagined.

In the one hundred and forty plus years that people have been climb-

Modern equipment.

ing Mount Baker, many thousands have attempted the ascent. The sport of mountaineering exploded in popularity in the late twentieth century, and new techniques and tools allowed climbers to venture into ever more challenging terrain everywhere. They have moved on to more difficult rock walls, frozen waterfalls, and obscure peaks in the North Cascades and other great ranges of the world. So many climbers traipse up the Coleman-Deming Glacier and Easton Glacier routes on Mount Baker at the Peak of the season that some years they wear a track in the snow visible with the naked eye from many miles distant. The exploits of these multitudes may not be historic, but they are certainly of great personal significance to every climber who overcomes the physical and sometimes emotional challenges of the experience. A few climbers stand out in the history of the mountain: Coleman, Morovits, Lee, Beckey and Cooper among them. These men were all pioneers, overcoming barriers, and exploring new ground and new possibilities. The opportunity for the sort of exploration they did on this mountain will not come again, but people will find new and exciting ways to experience the mountain, and everyone will explore their personal frontiers. In this respect Baker has become a different mountain and will continue to evolve in human experience of it.

11

Accidents and Rescues

When man knows how to live dangerously, he is not afraid to die.
When he is not afraid to die, he is, strangely, free to live.
                                                    – William O. Douglas, 1950

Fear gripped Edmund T. Coleman on that day in 1868 when he, Tennant and Ogilvy watched Thomas Stratton stride confidently across the glacier without benefit of rope or companion. He knew, as perhaps Stratton did not, what perils lurked on the ice for the unprepared. The principal threat to Stratton was the hidden crevasse. A smooth, seemingly innocent expanse of snow could be a death trap, sections of it merely inches thick where winter snow melting from the surface downward remains a thin bridge over a crack that may be a hundred feet deep. If Stratton happened to step in such a place, down he would go, perhaps to fatal injury in the fall, perhaps to a slower death from hypothermia in the icy cavern. What bothered Coleman and many experienced climbers since was not only the danger to Stratton, but its avoidability. His party had laboriously carried ropes up the mountain to minimize the threat of just such a glacial plunge.

Stratton's enthusiasm was not his undoing, but others over the years have not been so fortunate. Mount Baker has, as some would say it, been a "killer." Twenty one people have died on the mountain since Coleman's initial climb. Many others have been injured. Still others have had narrow escapes. Mishaps have also occurred on other mountains in the region. Some people took the risks of the high mountains casually, an attitude that reached its peak with the marathons. These races dramatized dangers so that such casualness was reduced, but it has always been present to some degree, with unhappy results.

Is it correct to say that Mount Baker is a killer? Such a view imputes malicious intent to an inanimate mountain of rock and ice. The story of accidents and tragedies on any mountain is one of "objective" dangers – the fall of rocks, ice or snow, the occurrence of sudden storms – and "subjective" dan-

C.C. Wright (left) and J.C. Bishop.

gers, those created by the mental and physical conditions of climbers, their judgment, training, preparation, and skill. Some accidents might have been avoided by a more fit and experienced person; some could not because circumstances brought a person and a falling block of ice together at a particular moment. In either case, the mountain is not responsible.

Many observers who themselves do not venture up onto the high mountains argue that the mistake leading to a mishap was made when the climber traveled up into the area of risk. If someone knows there is a risk, these observers contend, then the reasonable thing to do is avoid the situation entirely. They cannot fathom why anyone would voluntarily put themselves at risk. The entire story of Mount Baker exploration, of all mountaineering, is that of people seeking a challenge. Flirting with danger, mastering a situation full of hazards is a thrilling and fulfilling experience for many people. The rewards balance the potential costs. The compensation is spiritual and personal, not material. And there always seem to be people seeking such intangibles. Climbers have calculated the risks of Mount Baker, gambled with the odds. Most have won and a few have lost.

Early Mount Baker climbers had close calls. On his second attempt Coleman was forced to bivouac high on the mountain, as were Glisan and Lee and later Easton and his companions. They performed well, luck was with them, and they escaped without injury. The first death related to mountaineering (Dick Smith's death by his own rifle excepted) was J.C. Bishop in July of 1913. Bishop was an experienced mountaineer who had been the first President of the British Columbia Mountaineering Club, an office he held for three years. He was climbing Mount Baker to warm up for an extended venture into the Canadian Rockies. C.C. Wright, an early resident of Glacier, was climbing with him when the accident occurred. The two had climbed to the summit and were descending Roosevelt Glacier (the part of the glacier where the mishap occurred later was found to be a separate glacier and was named for Coleman) when Bishop plunged into a hidden crevasse. Some accounts claim he inadvertently stepped backward into the crevasse while taking a picture. Regardless of what caused his fall, Bishop became wedged head down in the narrow bottom of the crevasse. Wright, who barely escaped falling in himself, was unable to extricate him. Bishop may have died from the fall or from hypothermia; the record is unclear. Wright rushed down the mountain for help, but Bishop was dead long before rescuers reached him.

Bishop's accident occurred just before the running of the third Mount Baker Marathon. Little note of the incident appeared in Bellingham newspa-

Evacuation of Galbraith, 1913.

pers, perhaps because the victim was not a local man, perhaps because boosters were concerned that it might cast a cloud over the race or even result in its cancellation. By 1913 some people were concerned enough to publicly question the wisdom of the race. Despite Bishop's death the third race was held, and Victor Galbraith nearly met the same fate. Luck was with him, but the two incidents provided dramatic evidence of the dangers of climbing the mountain, and the marathon was ended. Efforts were made to revive the race in later years, but each time the hazards cited were sufficient reason not to do so.

Twenty-six years passed before another fatal accident occurred on the mountain. Many climbers ventured up during these years, but most did so in highly organized groups. The safety-consciousness of the time was reflected in the Mount Baker Club's newsletter. It stated unequivocally that the club was opposed to student climbers, who went on climbs without proper guides and organization. Further, the club disapproved of climbs in which less than three persons participated. These admonitions may have been prompted by the small parties that were venturing onto Baker in the late 1920s, principally from northeast of the mountain, where the Mount Baker Lodge was in full swing.

The next fatal accident, and the worst tragedy to occur in Mount Baker's climbing history, befell a large and well-organized party led by experienced guides. Since 1917, college students and faculty from Western Washington College of Education (now Western Washington University) had made an annual outing to the mountain. They had come in large groups, climbing the mountain each year, and had never encountered any problems. They would hike up the Glacier Trail to Kulshan Cabin, make the ascent up Coleman Glacier to the saddle, then climb the upper Deming Glacier to the summit. Everyone was given instruction in the use of ice axes and proper procedures for safe climbing. They felt prepared and had been successful year after year.

On Saturday, July 22, 1939, twenty-five climbers from the college began their ascent before dawn, according to normal procedure. Two Mount Baker veterans were leading. Don Coss was guide and Chet Ullin was his assistant. All went well as the party made its way over Coleman Glacier. Storms had dumped new snow on the higher reaches of the peak, but it had settled and seemed to offer no problems. Such storms are normal any time of the year on the upper mountain, and on the day of the climb the weather was clear and beautiful.

As the morning wore on, the sun shone brightly and people stripped off jackets and sweaters because of the heat. Everyone was climbing well as the party reached the last steep section of the upper Deming Glacier. They were perhaps fifteen minutes from the summit plateau, spread out in single file climbing straight up the steep slope, when their exultation turned to terror.

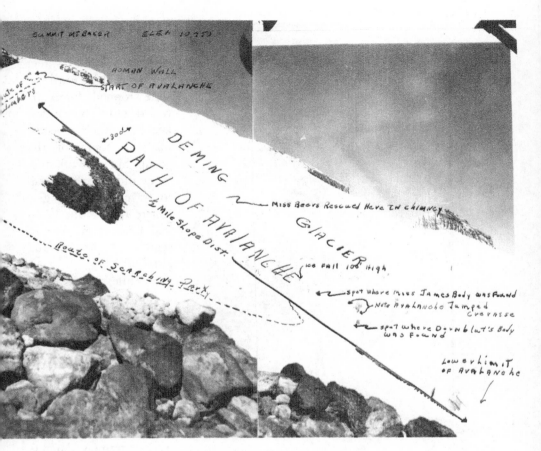

Diagram of 1939 accident that claimed six lives.

All of a sudden there was a swishing sound and a fine layer of loose snow began to sluff off the steep slope, gaining in thickness as it continued. The party was at the upper end of the sliding snow and before they knew it the members found themselves all sliding with it as though they were standing on a moving carpet. Some of them lost their balance right away and a shout went out from one of the guides to "Dig in!" This they did only to find that when they sunk their alpenstocks and ice axes into the moving snow, the force of the slide bent them over from the firm snow underneath as though they were blades of grass. Some swam, some crawled, but all of them were down, then up again, all fighting to move upwards so the sliding snow would all finally pass underneath them.[1]

189

view of Lower CREVASSE INTO WHicH
Dornbluts Body Fell. Note Depth gSnow
Fall. Probably 40-50 Feet AVALANche Snow
slid into This crevasse

The entire party of twenty-five were carried hundreds of feet down the slope until the slide stopped. Everyone was dazed. The guides, keeping their heads, made a count of the group. Six were missing. They ordered the group to traverse off the glacier to the saddle. Ullin and Coss then went in search of the missing climbers.

While the two guides were searching for survivors, the rest of the party waited in the saddle. They did not go out onto the glacier to search for their missing companions because conditions at the terminus of the avalanche were extremely dangerous. Small slides continued to come down the slope, and Coss and Ullin feared that someone else would be injured. Everyone was deeply shaken and their judgment perhaps affected by their narrow escape, so the two guides did their best.

The slide had finally stopped when it reached a crevassed area of Deming Glacier, just below the level of the saddle. It had poured over two ice cliffs and gone into a huge crevasse. The two searchers worked among the cliffs and crevasses for three hours, joined after a while by the two most experienced members of the climbing party. One woman was quickly rescued. A second was uncovered three hours after she had been buried. Ullin worked frantically to save her, giving her artificial respiration for one and a half hours, but could not revive her. Finally, as the afternoon waned and hope of finding anyone else alive diminished, dejected and exhausted searchers gave up and set off down the mountain for Kulshan Cabin. Other head counts revealed that seven students had initially been missing. One had been rescued, one was known to be dead. Five were missing.

At 8 p.m. two members of the party reported the accident to District Ranger William Parke at the Glacier Ranger Station. He pulled together a rescue party which included himself, three other Forest Service employees, and six CCC enrollees. They made the ten-mile hike to Kulshan Cabin with flashlights, arriving there at 3 a.m. Refreshed by a brief rest and breakfast, the rescue group, accompanied by Coss and Ullin, headed upward at 5:30. They reached the saddle and were examining the avalanche when three more volunteer searchers caught up with them. This brought the rescue group to fifteen.

Three people took the body of Alice James, uncovered the previous afternoon, down the mountain in an improvised canvas toboggan, and the twelve others entered the slide area and resumed probing and searching. Soon they found another body, Julius Dornblut, Jr., buried under three feet of snow. It had passed through a chute between seracs, dropped a hundred feet over an ice wall, and gone seventy feet into a crevasse. Dornblut's location confirmed the fears of the searchers that other missing students were probably buried deep in the large crevasse.

They worked through the day but found no one else, finally returning to Kulshan Cabin exhausted from their labors and sleepless night. The search went on for thirteen days but no more bodies were ever found. Deming Glacier is the final resting place of Hope Weitman, Beulah Lindberg, Maynard Howat and Vene Fisher.

Much debate marked the aftermath of this tragedy about whether the accident could have been avoided. Most informed people concluded that it could not. Midsummer snowstorms are common on the mountain; in Baker's entire climbing history there have been only two recorded incidents like this one (the other a fatality in the same place in late summer of 1979). Coss and Ullin judged the snow stable enough to travel on. Perhaps they did not expect the temperature to be quite as warm as it turned out to be, with the summer sun beating directly onto the steep slope and its fresh snow. The party was large and may have been climbing too slowly. Hindsight raises many factors that contributed to the tragedy. At the time and "on the ground," guides saw no cause for alarm and were following established procedures on a commonly climbed route. Circumstances conspired to bring down the unusually large avalanche that ran far enough to bury the unfortunate students.

Five years after the college group's mishap, another fatality occurred in August, 1944. Two young members of The Mountaineers from Seattle were taking their summer "tour" of the mountains. Larry Strathdee and Jack

Schwabland, ages sixteen and seventeen, climbed Glacier Peak and then came up to Mount Baker. Confident of good weather and a speedy ascent, they hiked the trail to Boulder Ridge with light packs, leaving even their sleeping bags in their car.

Their climb up the ridge and glacier went smoothly, and at noon they neared the summit. Here they were faced with a decision – they could stay on the glacier and climb easily onto the summit, or they could go up a steep slope of ice above the bergschrund, which would lead to crumbly rock cliffs up which they could climb to the top. Larry insisted they should go the hard way. Jack was not for the idea and finally Jack refused to go up the ice, so Larry set out to do it alone. Climbing unroped and not even bothering to cut steps, he lost his footing and slid down steep ice toward the bergschrund. Unable to slow his fall with his ax, he shot over the schrund, hit the lower lip fifty feet below, then slid another two hundred feet down steep ice before stopping.

Jack traversed over to his badly injured companion. They were in a fix. Help was many hours away. They had no sleeping bag to protect Larry from hypothermia. No one could help the injured man while Jack went for help. Jack did what he could, giving Larry all the clothing he could spare and making him as comfortable as possible though he could not move him off the ice.

Jack raced down the mountain, reaching the ranger station near Baker Lake at 8 p.m. A rescue party was organized, but it was late the next afternoon before it reached the scene of the accident. They found Larry dead from a combination of head injuries, shock, and hypothermia. Mount Baker had claimed a young man who had underestimated the challenge and overestimated his ability.

Eighteen more years passed and hundreds of people safely climbed the mountain. Then in November of 1962, Hans Jorritsma, a South African, and Joan Huckell of Sydney, Australia, approached the mountain along Ptarmigan Ridge, bent on climbing Park Glacier. Huckell apparently was not up to the climb, so Jorritsma left her on or near Rainbow Glacier, a flat, small glacier near the northeastern base of the peak. He proceeded alone, climbing above the Cockscomb to a point some two hundred feet below the summit. The weather was excellent, but November days are short. Lacking crampons and forced to cut hundreds of steps on the rock hard headwall of Park Glacier, Jorritsma ran out of time and turned around just short of the summit.

Rejoining Huckell, they roped up and proceeded toward the Portals, a formation of rock pinnacles that flanks the access to Park Glacier. Somewhere near the West Portal Jorritsma slipped and pulled Huckell down with him. The two slid a short distance, the woman sliding into rocks and sustaining head and chest injuries. Jorritsma was unhurt but Huckell had difficulty breathing and could barely walk, so they struggled to the edge of the glacier and bivouacked in the moat.

The fall occurred at about 3 p.m. Jorritsma stayed with his injured partner until 3 a.m. when he finally decided he had to go for help. Instead of going out Ptarmigan Ridge to the Mount Baker Ski Area, Jorritsma took what he thought was a shortcut directly down Wells Creek. Many hours later an exhausted Jorritsma reached the Mount Baker Highway and got a ride to the Glacier Ranger Station.

In his exhaustion he reported that his injured partner was on the trail. Thinking this meant rescuers might reach her in the remaining daylight, the Forest Service enlisted the help of Dr. Otto Trott, a veteran climber who was working on his cabin near Glacier, and thirteen Marine reservists who were in the area on a training exercise. The sixteen men (one Forest Service man and Jorritsma went along) drove to the trailhead near Table Mountain, and set out along Ptarmigan Ridge.

The weather had changed dramatically. Heavy snow was falling and high winds battered the exposed ridge. The rescue party reached Camp Kiser, just beyond which the trail ends, and found that they were still a long way from the injured woman. The marines were dressed in cotton pants and long parkas, and no one in the party was prepared to spend a night exposed to such severe weather. They had no choice but to retreat to a stand of trees, build a fire and tend to their own survival.

At daylight the storm still raged as they set out again. They were overtaken by a rescue team from the Seattle Mountain Rescue Council but even this augmented and experienced group had trouble finding Huckell. Visibility was very poor, and Jorritsma had trouble locating the spot where he had left her. Finally at noon, two nights and forty five hours after the accident, they reached the bivouac site. Huckell was dead, her body covered with one and a half feet of new snow. Conditions were too severe to remove her body, so the team left it there intending to come back for it when the weather allowed. A series of storms buried the area and not until the following July was a Bellingham Mountain Rescue team able to retrieve the remains of the unfortunate woman.

Another fatal incident occurred in 1969. On May 25 four young Canadians skied up the Coleman Glacier, as many dedicated skiers do to extend their season in late spring and early summer. Ski areas were closed for the season so the group fastened climbing skins to their skis and made their way up to the saddle, not intending to climb to the summit. The weather seemed good and the hour early, so they decided to bag the peak before their run down the mountain.

Leaving their skis and packs just above the saddle, they took their ski poles and started upward, climbing in their ski boots. As sometimes happens this early in the year, the weather suddenly changed. Clouds blew in, visibility was reduced, the wind rose, and the temperature dropped quickly. On their descent from the summit the entire group, roped together, fell and slid over a rock cliff. John Dallmeyer, the only experienced climber in the group, was killed. Judy Small was injured. Mario Strim and Margaret Secrett survived the fall unscathed.

Strim and Secrett dug a snow hole, probably with their hands, placed the injured woman in it to shield her from the icy wind. They then huddled together nearby, struggling for warmth as a storm raged on the mountain. By next morning all were dead, Small from a combination of trauma and hypothermia, the other two from hypothermia. The group was reported missing, but because of the storm it was several days before rescue teams were able to reach the scene of the accident.

Here was a disaster caused by subjective factors. Certainly a storm blew in, but had the party set off downward immediately, they probably would have escaped. Their climbing equipment was inadequate, though many climb to the summit similarly ill-equipped with no problems. Ski poles are no substitute for ice axes in arresting a fall. They may have slipped on the descent because they were climbing in ski boots. Most disastrously, they ventured up onto a big mountain without adequate clothing or emergency equipment and did so at a time of the year when rapid changes in weather are not uncommon. Starting their day in deceptively warm and sunny spring conditions, they were surprised by the change and being ill-prepared gave them no margin for error. They paid the ultimate price for this.

The incidents described give a sense of how people have gotten into trouble on Mount Baker over the years. Other serious accidents have occurred on the mountain, too numerous to describe in such detail. A University of Washington student died in 1973 when, inadequately dressed, he became hypothermic on a climb of the Coleman Headwall. The summer of 1979 was a disastrous one. A single crevasse claimed two lives in separate accidents, and in August a fatality occurred on Deming Glacier in a situation much like that of the 1939 avalanche disaster. Mountain rescue teams were on the mountain weekly from mid-July through August. A fatality occurred on New Years Day 1981 low on the mountain near Kulshan Cabin. One woman died and two men were seriously injured when they fell while skiing in extremely icy conditions. Most recently, a young man, Kevin LaFleur, disappeared inexplicably on a solo early season ski ascent in perfect conditions. He was likely claimed by an unexpected and undetected crevasse, and no sign of him has been found.

This litany of injury and death must be balanced by another side of the story – all mishaps do not end in the death of the victim. People are often rescued – by their own party, by other climbers, or by rescue teams. Rescues far outnumber fatalities, and there have been some dramatic, even heroic rescues over the years. It is testimony to the skill, dedication, and perseverance of mountain rescuers that few lives have been lost in over a century of human endeavor on the mountain.

One rescue, in October of 1979, had all the elements of a well-oiled rescue operation on a big, glaciated Northwest mountain. The story began when experienced climbers descending Coleman Glacier encountered a pair of young novice climbers camped below the Black Buttes. The two young men proudly proclaimed they were going to climb the Coleman Headwall; they would not be dissuaded by the more experienced climbers, who pointed out that this was not a beginner's climb any time of the year – in October when ice was exposed and snow frozen rock hard it was a challenge even for experts. The climbers who spoke with the youths were so concerned that when they came off the mountain they reported their encounter to the Whatcom County Sheriff, who coordinates all rescue work in the region. They believed a serious problem might be imminent. This initial report was made late Saturday.

Sunday began as a nice day, but gradually the weather deteriorated. By nightfall a strong storm was blasting the mountain. Heavy rain and high winds buffeted the lowlands throughout the night and Monday while snow fell on higher elevations. The two young climbers had signed in for the climb at the Glacier Ranger Station but had not signed out by Monday evening. The Saturday prediction was fulfilled, and a rescue operation was initiated. The decision to start the rescue machinery rests with the deputy sheriff in charge of search and rescue, who is advised by the Bellingham Mountain Rescue Council. The initial report of the potential problem, the bad weather, and the climbers' failure to sign out gave ample reason to begin a rescue operation.

By dawn on Tuesday a team of rescuers stood on the moraine below Coleman Glacier sorting equipment. They were from the Bellingham and Seattle Mountain Rescue Councils and had traveled through the night to be ready to search at dawn. The weather was clear and very cold. Six inches of new snow lay over the rocks of the moraine and the rock-hard ice of the glacier. A cold wind blew snow across the ice, creating at times a knee-deep ground blizzard. Since the missing climbers could be anywhere on the mountain, the small force was to spread out in rope teams and work their way up Coleman Glacier to the base of the headwall, looking into crevasses as they went.

As the teams started up, the thud of helicopter rotors broke the wintery stillness. A large "bird" from the Whidbey Island Naval Air Station had picked up a Bellingham Mountain Rescue observer and was to inspect the headwall. As the rescuers on the ground ventured slowly onto the glacier, the chopper flew slowly back and forth across the face. The helicopter crew spotted the missing climbers' tent, or what was left of it after the storm. There was no sign of life around the camp, and they found nothing on the face. The aircraft dropped the observer off on the Glacier Creek road, and flew back to its base to refuel.

Meanwhile on the glacier, Al Errington and Joe Kasuba of Seattle Mountain Rescue examined several crevasses then sat down several feet from the lip of a large one for a rest and a snack. As they sat there, the snow under them suddenly cracked off and thundered into the crevasse, throwing the two backward forty feet down into the glacier. Errington righted himself. His back had been sprained in the fall, but no bones had been broken. He looked around for Joe in the jumble of ice blocks that had fallen into the crevasse but could only see the rope disappearing among them. At first he thought that Joe had been buried, perhaps crushed.

Fortunately, however, Joe had also landed on top of the debris but had been more seriously injured. Al soon found him, located the radio the two were carrying, and called for help. All rescue teams abandoned the search for the missing climbers and converged on the crevasse. Al and Joe's fellow Seattle team members climbed into the crevasse to help with Joe's injuries; the Bellingham Mountain Rescue team tackled the problem of preparing for a helicopter evacuation of the victims.

The slope below the crevasse dropped off moderately to other crevasses 150 feet below. A slip down the slope would end in one of these crevasses, so great care had to be taken in moving around. A fixed rope was set up to allow safe movement along the lower lip of the crevasse where the rescuers were working. The helicopter returned from its refueling run and flew up to the accident site. First it attempted to lower a medical corpsman, but rescuers frantically waved the chopper away from the crevasse for fear that concussion of the rotor blades would knock down more debris. A huge block of snow and ice was wedged into the crevasse; a fairly easy evacuation could be made by traversing beneath this block to where the crevasse floor (actually a snow bridge) rose to the surface of the glacier. If the block collapsed it would not only endanger the rescuers but would necessitate a much more complex procedure to raise the injured man to where he could be lifted by the helicopter. The corpsman, a member of the U.S. Navy helicopter crew, was lowered on the end of a steel cable to the hard icy slope west of the accident site. He had no crampons or ice axe, only his slick-soled boots. Rescuers could see that the

Whidbey Island Naval Air helicopter lowers Bellingham Mountain Rescue crew onto glacier.

Bellingham Mountain Rescue member.

moment he released himself from the cable he would slide down the slope into a crevasse so they tried to wave him off. Rescuers on the ground and in the chopper were on different radio frequencies and could not communicate directly. The pilot finally understood the situation and took their advice. He flew away with the corpsman dangling on the end of the cable, which was jammed. The crew eventually managed to haul him back into the ship. Meanwhile, the ice block stayed in place.

Again the helicopter came back, this time lowering a litter to several climbers who had anchored themselves to the mountainside well away from the crevasse where Joe was being cared for. They caught the litter, dragged it across the steep slope to the crevasse, and Joe was placed in it. He was in great pain from multiple injuries, and his condition was becoming serious. The litter was gingerly moved along the crevasse, under the ice block and up to the glacier's surface. Again the chopper came up, the blast from its rotors creating a hurricane. Blowing snow made visibility almost nil. Despite these blizzard conditions, the cable was lowered and attached to the litter, and Joe was lifted off the glacier. As the machine hovered, a great thump was heard and felt as the ice block collapsed into the crevasse. Everyone was by now well away from it, and Joe was successfully raised into the helicopter and flown to the hospital in Bellingham. He recovered from his injuries.

The original pair of climbers whom everyone had come to assist were still missing. The ground searchers came off the glacier, exhausted by the effort to save one of their own, and the helicopter flew back over the mountain for more aerial searching. They found nothing. Volunteers driving the Middle Fork Road finally came upon the two exhausted youths.

Despite their inexperience, the two had successfully climbed the Coleman Headwall on Sunday in deteriorating weather. Their intention was to descend Deming Glacier and then Coleman Glacier to their tent, but in the blowing mist and snow they became confused and descended the eastern side of the mountain instead. They reached timberline as the full force of the storm hit the mountain, and they spent Sunday night there, wet and cold, but sheltered. Instead of continuing downward to Baker Lake, they tried to traverse back south and west around the mountain, undoubtedly intending to return to their tent. They endured two more nights before they finally were discovered – tired, cold and hungry but uninjured. Their navigation skills had failed them, but their survival skills had been exceptional.

The accident that befell the rescuers is a perfect example of an unavoidable objective occurrence. The tons of ice that broke off had probably been poised to do so for days, and the two rescuers just happened to be there when it did. Perhaps their weight, though inconsequential in relation to the weight of the ice, tipped the balance. They had been placed in that spot by the miscalculations of the young climbers they were trying to rescue. Ironically, the experienced rescuers were hurt while the novices were unscathed. The two youths probably never gave the possibility of rescue a thought when plotting their adventure. Rescue teams seldom mind being called out to assist people who have been unlucky or who have erred, but this incident indicates what is at stake when a rescue effort is necessary.

The story of every rescue on the mountain involves the hard realities of life and death. On Mount Baker, people rise to great heights, literally and figuratively, but they rise to a place beyond the relative safety and insulation of daily life. That is why they go up there – to encounter and struggle with the elements. Usually they win the struggle and are better for it. Sometimes they do not.

My grandmothers are full of memories, smelling of soap and onions and wet clay, with veins rolling roughly over quick hands, they have many clean words to say. My grandmothers were strong.

– Margaret Walker

Common Weights and Measures

1 tablespoon (tbsp)=3 teaspoons (tsp)

1/16 cup = 1 tablespoon
1/8 cup = 2 tablespoons
1/6 cup = 2 tablespoons + 2 teaspoons
1/4 cup = 4 tablespoons
1/3 cup=5 tablespoons + 1 teaspoon
3/8 cup = 6 tablespoons
1/2 cup = 8 tablespoons
2/3 cup=10 tablespoons + 2 teaspoons
3/4 cup = 12 tablespoons
1 cup = 48 teaspoons
1 cup = 16 tablespoons
8 fluid ounces (fl oz) = 1 cup
1 pint (pt) = 2 cups
1 quart (qt) = 2 pints
4 cups = 1 quart
1 gallon (gal) = 4 quarts
16 ounces (oz) = 1 pound (lb)

U.S. to Metric

1/5 teaspoon = 1 milliliter
1 teaspoon = 5 ml
1 tablespoon = 15 ml
1 fluid oz = 30 ml
1/5 cup = 47 ml
1 cup = 237 ml
2 cups (1 pint) = 473 ml
4 cups (1 quart) = .95 liter
4 quarts (1 gal.) = 3.8 liters

Metric to U.S.

1 milliliter = 1/5 teaspoon
5 ml = 1 teaspoon
15 ml = 1 tablespoon
100 ml = 3.4 fluid oz
240 ml = 1 cup
1 liter = 34 fluid oz. 4.2 cups

Celsius to Farenheit

$0°C = 32 °F$
$5°C = 41 °F$
$10°C = 50 °F$
$15°C = 59 °F$
$20°C = 68 °F$
$25°C = 77 °F$
$30°C = 86 °F$
$35°C = 95 °F$
$40°C = 104 °F$
$45°C = 113 °F$
$50°C = 122 °F$
$55°C = 131 °F$
$60°C = 140 °F$
$65°C = 149 °F$
$70°C = 158 °F$
$75°C = 167 °F$
$80°C = 176 °F$
$85°C = 185 °F$
$90°C = 194 °F$
$95°C = 203 °F$
$100°C = 212 °F$

BRAMBLE & BERRY

SOAP MAKING SUPPLIES

12

The Land of Many Uses

National parks should be relatively spacious land and water areas so outstanding and superior in quality and beauty as to make imperative their preservation by the Federal Government for the enjoyment, education, and inspiration of all people.

— National Park Service pamphlet, 1972

The Mount Baker country has long been noted for the unsurpassed value of its natural resources. The mountain itself, with its glaciers and subalpine meadows, is of unexcelled scenic value. Dark green tree-covered slopes sweep up through light green alpine meadows draped like a garment over ridges to the perpetually white dome of the glaciated summit. Tall trees of great timber value cover the lower slopes and valleys around the mountain. Even the rocks are valuable, as miners and prospectors have testified for a century and a half. Waters that flow from the snow and ice nurture fish, float rafters, and provide hydroelectric power. The region is prime recreation country, a place for fishing, hunting, climbing, skiing, or simply sitting beneath a great fir tree and contemplating the wonder of it all. As the twentieth century passed and the press of human needs and wants in the region grew, debate about how to best use and manage these resource riches also increased.

Very early in the century, as has been noted, some groups believed that the Mount Baker region's great value lay in its scenery and recreational potential. If this could be developed, they argued, it would prove a great boon to all of northwestern Washington. Development proceeded, but a great national depression and then a world war intervened, and development failed to yield the fruits that many expected. After the war, the nation's economy boomed, and demand for lumber for construction increased markedly. Recreation demand increased as well, and the Unites States Forest Service was challenged to meet the growing and often competing demands of diverse constituencies for the resources in their care. Satisfying public demands had never been easy when the population was sparse and demands light; it became ever more difficult as the nation prospered and the population grew.

The Mount Baker region, as earlier described, was made a forest reserve in 1897 and administered by the Department of the Interior. Then, in 1905, the reserve was transferred to the jurisdiction of the Department of Agriculture. Between 1910 and 1917 the Mazamas and other groups advocated for a national park, which if realized would have moved the region back into the Department of the Interior. The original park plan was scuttled by World War I, but this did not end the argument over who should administer the area and for what purpose. The debate continued, sometimes heating up and reaching public attention and the ears of legislators in Washington, D.C. The history of this debate is important to understanding the current situation on and around Mount Baker and its future prospects.

In 1917, prior to the United States entering World War I, hearings were held to consider Mount Baker National Park bills introduced in the Sixty-fifth U.S. Congress, and there was much support for them. The Departments of Agriculture and Interior reported to congressional committees: Agriculture was solidly against a park, Interior solidly for it. The war intervened and stalled the park initiative, but after the war bills were reintroduced into the Sixty-sixth Congress. Once again they died in committee. The pro-park forces had exhausted their resources and energy in their pre-war promotion. National park politics were also changing with the newly established National Park Service getting its bearings. Whatever the reason, no action was taken on the park proposals, and the Mount Baker National Park idea went back into incubation. The Forest Service went about the business of extending its supervision and control of the Mount Baker National Forest.

In 1926 the Secretary of Agriculture established the Mount Baker Park Division of the Forest. This division, which came to be known as the Mount Baker Recreation Area, encompassed 74,859 acres. The designation gave recognition to the exceptional recreational value of the peak and its surrounding ridges and valleys. The Forest Service, at this point beginning a long political and bureaucratic competition with the emergent and ambitious National Park Service over which public lands should become national parks, established this designation to thwart national park ambitions in the region. The Mount Baker Lodge was soon to open, and everyone was most enthusiastic about the future of recreation at Heather Meadows and elsewhere on and around Mount Baker. The Forest Service cooperated fully with the Mount Baker Development Company that was building the lodge, and everyone seemed satisfied with the agency's management. Establishment of the recreation area would allow logging, mining, and water development projects in the "protected" division, as long as such projects did not impair its recreational values.

Everyone's interests would be served, and the Forest Service hoped it would not be bothered by further park proposals.

All was quiet for eight years until the Bellingham Chamber of Commerce adopted a resolution in 1934 calling for a park of 74,759 acres, to include both Mount Baker and Mount Shuksan. Once again the intent of the proposal was "toward developing the recreational advantages of the district."[1] Bert Huntoon presented the resolution, which in part pointed out that

> under the laws and regulations governing the administration of national forests, the national forest service has very limited funds and no organization to develop adequate facilities for the convenience, pleasure and comfort of the tourist . . . whereas, the national park service has the funds, organization and facilities to develop and make adequate use of the said area for national recreation purposes and to administer the same.[2]

Progress toward full recreational development had slowed at Heather Meadows and in the Mount Baker region generally, due largely to the Depression. At the same time, the National Park Service had emerged as the national leader in promoting outdoor recreation. Undoubtedly the Bellingham Chamber sought a stimulant for its developmental aspirations and thought it would have a better chance of achieving them with the Park Service. Or, perhaps its park advocacy would motivate the Forest Service to pay more attention to recreation. Ironically the Forest Service, with the extensive labor of the Civilian Conservation Corps available, was beginning the greatest effort in recreation development that the area was ever to experience.

Nothing came of the Chamber resolution, though interest in national park status for the Mount Baker area was reviving in other quarters. That same year the Land Planning Committee of the Natural Resources Board proposed national park status for several of the most scenic volcanic peaks in Washington, Mount Baker among them. Three years later the Director of the National Park Service appointed a special committee to investigate the park potential of the Cascades. This committee's report recommended a massive park of five thousand square miles which would include all of the major volcanoes in Washington State from Baker in the north to Mount Adams and Mount St. Helens in the south. This proposal came to be known as "Ice Peaks National Park" and raised a storm of protest. Miners, loggers and diverse others interested in exploiting the resources of the Cascades protested that their business would be severely curtailed, if not eliminated, were such vast acreage devoted to a park. The purpose of a national park is in part, after all, to preserve and protect the beauty and integrity of natural areas, and the proponents of development rightly saw such protection as incompatible with their aspirations. In response to their concerns the National Park Service, the Forest Service and the Washington State Planning council all launched more studies of the Cascades. Public hearings were held, and in 1940 the National Park Service submitted another report which called for a Cascades National Park. It would include the glacier-bearing peaks, Mount Baker among them, though it was not on the same grand scale as the 1938 proposal. The Forest Service, not surprisingly, endorsed continuing Forest Service management and opposed any park proposals. The Washington State Planning Council also opposed any parks in the Cascades.

This flurry of proposals and studies revealed a conflict that was to characterize all future discussion of Cascade mountain resource policies. In the cover letter to its "Cascade Mountain Study," the Chairman of the Washington State Planning Council noted the Council's opposition to National Park Service management of the North Cascades: "If either plan were adopted, large areas would no doubt be removed from the forest reserves and their wealth of forest and other natural resources would either be completely locked up or their development seriously hampered."[3] From this moment on in the resource management debate it would be the developers versus the preservers. Until the Ice Peaks proposal was unveiled, many proponents of national park status for Mount Baker had themselves been developers, though their interest had been primarily recreational development. They had also been local people. The state's study, however, indicated that people living near the mountains were concerned for the future of "abundant natural resources," that they were entering a "phase of discovery and development" and that they wanted minimal interference from the Federal Government in their efforts to develop what they might discover in the Federal domain.[4]

World War II reduced interest in new parks, and Mount Baker remained in the National Forest. Twenty years passed, during which the Forest Service managed the Mount Baker region under a multiple-use policy. Investment was made in recreational development during this time, but it was also a period of increased emphasis on timber production. Roads were extended or built in valleys around the mountain, and clearcuts appeared along these advancing thoroughfares. Throughout the Cascade Range, extensive road building and logging were the rule, and as the 1950s progressed, concern rose in some quarters that the scenic and recreational values of the mountains were being sacrificed to "commodity production," the extraction of timber, minerals, and other natural resources.

This concern was heard in Washington, D.C., and in 1960 bills were introduced into the Eighty-sixth Congress to provide for studies by the Departments of Interior and Agriculture of the advisability of establishing a

Mount Baker.

national park in the central and northern Cascades. No congressional action was taken, and similar bills were introduced in the next session. Again there was no congressional action, but the Secretary of Agriculture stopped all logging and roadbuilding in twenty areas of the North Cascades until a high-mountain management policy could be written. Support for a national park in the North Cascades was growing.

A group of conservationists came together to form the North Cascades Conservation Council (NCCC). In 1963 they proposed a 1,038,665-acre North Cascades National Park and a 269,521-acre Chelan National Mountain Recreation Area. Mount Baker was not included in their proposal.[5] That same year a "new era of cooperation" between the traditionally antagonistic Departments of the Interior and Agriculture was announced in a joint letter to President Kennedy from the department secretaries. Among proposals for cooperation was a joint study "of the Federal lands in the North Cascade Mountains of Washington to determine the management and administration of those lands that will best serve the public interest."[6] A study team was soon appointed to visit the mountains, hold public hearings and issue a report.

The team's "North Cascades Study Report," issued in 1965, recommended establishment of four new wilderness areas (the Wilderness Act, passed by Congress the previous September, provided for establishment of a National Wilderness Preservation System), a North Cascades National Park including Mount Shuksan, additions to Mount Rainier National Park, and development of a system of scenic roads. One road was recommended to go from Heather Meadows to Baker Lake through a tunnel under Austin Pass. Mount Baker was excluded from the proposed park. The mountain "and most of the surrounding Recreation Area should continue to be administered by the Forest Service in accord with that agency's plans for development . . . ."[7]

The central goal of this exercise was to resolve the long-standing argument between the various groups and agencies vying for use and control of the high Cascades. The Study Team's recommendation was a compromise, and it failed to achieve that goal. The report included letters to the study team from George Selke, a consultant to the Secretary of Agriculture, and George B. Hartzog, Jr., Director of the National Park Service. These letters revealed a chasm that could not be bridged to resolve the central issues. Selke wrote that he was not pleased with the final recommendations, for he was opposed to the idea of any new national park in the State of Washington.

> Certainly, the Mount Baker and Mount Shuksan area has National Park quality. But would it serve the State and Nation better as a National Park than it does now as a full-year outdoor recreation

area . . . ? My contention is that the extreme northern part of the North Cascades, even Mt. Baker and Mt. Shuksan, have too short a season and too much inclement weather during three-fourths of the year to become a heavily patronized National Park. To become an outstanding recreation area, which it is now and we set aside to be 50 years ago, with year-round active outdoor recreation is still a wiser proposal.[8]

Selke thought the Forest Service should continue to manage the area.

Hartzog was not pleased with the Study Team's recommendations either, but for entirely different reasons.

I must . . . object strongly to your deletion of the Nooksack Valley. Especially, do I object strenuously to your deletion of Mount Baker.

. . . Your failure to include Mount Baker as we have recommended is even more startling and confusing when one realizes that, as long ago as 1926, the Secretary of Agriculture recognized the national significance and park-like character of Mount Baker by designating it the Mount Baker Park Division of the Mount Baker National Forest. Thus, for almost 40 years, by Secretarial Order, the Forest Service has given Mount Baker a special and unique management recognition of its superlative scenic and scientific values . . . .[9]

The report with its compromises satisfied no one and, despite Hartzog's passionate advocacy of including Mount Baker in any national park in the North Cascades, it was not to be.

On January 30, 1967, President Lyndon Johnson presented a message to the Ninetieth Congress recommending that it establish a national park in the North Cascades. Further work commenced on a legislative proposal, and in March a bill was introduced in the United States Senate to establish a national park in the North Cascades and Ross Lake National Recreation Area. After much debate and public testimony, a bill was passed in 1968, which established the park and several wilderness and recreation areas.[10] Right to the end, conservationists and the National Park Service urged that the proposed park be enlarged by 135,580 acres in the Mount Baker region. They failed, and the new park included Mount Shuksan but excluded the scenic Tomyhoi-Selesia areas with their mineral deposits (site of the Lone Jack and other claims) and the Mount Baker and Baker Lake region with its stands of timber. After nearly sixty years of discussion, the National Park Service assumed management of a significant portion of the North Cascades, but not of Mount Baker.

The argument over management of Mount Baker did not end with the decision to create a North Cascades National Park. During the years since that decision, which loggers and others hoped would resolve where they could and could not work, new issues and arguments have arisen. Decisions have been made by the Forest Service and by Congress that have achieved some of the goals of earlier Mount Baker park advocates, though not all. Use of the area for recreation in both summer and winter has grown dramatically. The Mount Baker Ski Area, descendant of the original Mount Baker Development Company's Mount Baker Lodge resort, has expanded extensively, adding runs and lifts, shifting the center of skiing from Heather Meadows to Shuksan Arm. In summer, day hikers, backpackers and climbers often crowd the trails while in winter back-country skiers, snowboarders, and snowmobilers travel trails and roads buried under deep snow. On pleasant summer or fall weekends, traffic jams the Artist Point and Heather Meadow area, and lines of hikers wind up and around Table Mountain.

The paramount issue since 1968 has been how to accommodate this high demand for recreation and scenic beauty with continuing demand for timber. How much of the Mount Baker country should be preserved in its wild state and allocated for wilderness recreation and how much should be logged? By the 1970s, a quarter of a million acres in the area remained wild, untouched by road or chainsaw. Throughout the United States, dozens of national forest areas were being studied and proposed (or often not) for addition to the National Wilderness Preservation System that Congress established in 1964. The Mount Baker area was not one of those mandated under the Wilderness Act for wilderness review, but because it was a large roadless area, a "de facto" wilderness, it became part of a national struggle to decide what parts of the national forest system should or should not be kept wild and roadless.

The Forest Service, pressed by new legislation and the threat of lawsuits, launched what it called its Roadless Area Review and Evaluation (RARE) from 1971-1973 to identify roadless, undeveloped areas in its domain and recommend to Congress areas it thought should be considered for inclusion in the National Wilderness Preservation System. The process involved public hearings and study of management alternatives for each roadless area.

Management alternatives were generated for the 275,000 roadless acres on and around Mount Baker and ranged from no wilderness to all wilderness. After hearings and study were complete, interested parties waited anxiously for the Forest Service decision, but no decision was made. The RARE process proved inadequate and its results inconclusive nationally, so no action

Mount Shuksan in winter.

came of it. Pressure was building on the Forest Service to decide what should be wilderness and what "released" to commodity producers, but criteria used in RARE were challenged as too general and some roadless areas were missed altogether. The Forest Service decided not to make specific recommendations for fear of litigation and decided further inventory was necessary, building on the work done in RARE. In the meantime, no new roads were built into roadless areas in the Mount Baker area, but where there were roads logs came out of the woods at an increasing rate. Pressure on the Forest Service to resolve the wilderness issue on Mount Baker and elsewhere continued to rise.

The next review process, which began in June 1977, was called RARE II. It identified 2,919 roadless areas in national forests nationwide, including parts of the Mount Baker region and the mountain itself. After considering various factors, including public comment, existing laws and regulations, identified public needs, and the professional judgment of its experts, the Forest

Service finally made its recommendations to the Secretary of Agriculture. Of the three alternatives that could be recommended for each area – wilderness, non-wilderness or future study – Mount Baker was declared non-wilderness.

One study after another had testified to the unique wild and scenic nature of Mount Baker and its surroundings. Yet once again, as had earlier occurred when compromise drew the boundaries of the North Cascades National Park Complex, any long-term protection of the wild and scenic values of the mountain was denied. Those who sought to protect their access to timber and minerals prevailed. Though this was the heyday of popular support for wilderness, the power of the timber industry in the region was considerable and tipped the scale against any wilderness recommendation for Mount Baker. This power, coupled with agency culture and politics elevated commercial forestry over dispersed recreation, scenery and wildness in this corner of the National Forest System. Multiple use would continue as the guiding philosophy of management for Mount Baker. The prospect of "release" of the timber resources in the region seemed imminent.

Still, the struggle was not over. Conservationists had not put much hope in the RARE process as a way to protect Mount Baker and had been organizing for an initiative of their own. Local activists had been inspired and encouraged by developments elsewhere in wilderness politics. One development was the shifting of initiative from government-driven wilderness preservation as in the RARE inventories to grassroots citizen-driven approaches.

In 1972 the Scapegoat Wilderness in Montana became the first "de facto" wilderness to enter the National Wilderness Preservation System, and it did so not by the initiative of the Forest Service but of citizen conservationists. A dedicated, persistent wilderness activist in Montana by the name of Cecil Garland formed the Lincoln Backcountry Protection Association, and ultimately succeeded in achieving congressional designation of a national forest wilderness. Garland's success inspired other citizen groups to launch campaigns for their favorite "de facto" wilderness, which was one factor that led the Forest Service to fear it was losing control of decisions about how its domain should be used. It launched its RARE inventories to get ahead of citizens pursuing their own wilderness proposals, but failed. The Scapegoat precedent encouraged citizen groups in Washington State such as the Alpine Lakes Protection Society, which in 1976 succeeded in achieving an Alpine Lakes Wilderness in the southern part of the North Cascades. These examples prompted a group of wilderness enthusiasts in the Bellingham area to form the Mount Baker Wilderness Association, and in 1980 the Association drew up a proposal for a 235,000 acre Mount Baker Wilderness.

A second change in wilderness politics came from a court decision in California which required that the Forest Service prepare an environmental

Mount Baker.

impact statement before areas of national forests in California, inventoried in RARE II and "released" from wilderness consideration, could be developed. Ironically this motivated the timber industry and other developers to press for legislation in other states to designate roadless areas as wilderness so the rest of the inventoried land could be released for development. Doug Scott, a player in all of this political maneuvering, describes what happened:

> Conservationists and their congressional champions . . . used this industry pressure as leverage. They insisted that any bills that would release some roadless lands from the court's requirement should also designate a substantial portion of the roadless lands as wilderness . . . . In short order Congress passed national forest wilderness-and-release package bills for many states. In 1984 alone Congress enacted such laws designating more than 8 million acres of new national forest wilderness areas in eighteen states.[11]

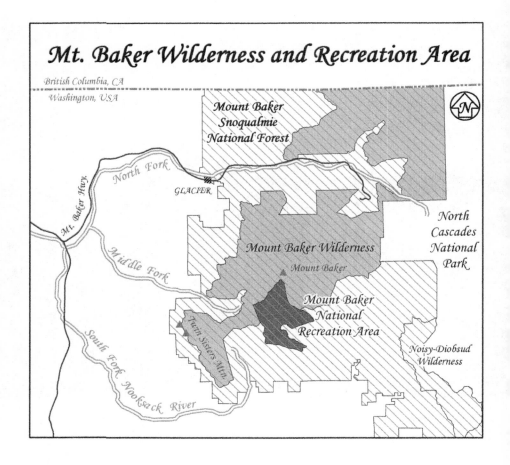

One of the "wilderness-and-release package bills" passed in 1984 was the Washington State Wilderness Act, and it included the 117,900-acre Mount Baker Wilderness and a Mount Baker National Recreation Area.

The Mount Baker Wilderness Association aimed initially for 235,000 acres of wilderness but achieved considerably less than that goal. As with all wilderness legislation there were issues to resolve and compromises to be made. In this case the boundaries of the wilderness were drawn to accommodate logging roads that had earlier been pushed up many major creeks around the mountain and north of the Mount Baker Highway. Where timber might be accessed from these roads, boundaries were drawn high toward timberline, as on Skyline Divide. A large, roadless area north of Canyon Creek along the Canadian Border was excluded. Perhaps the most painful compromise for wilderness advocates was creation in the legislation of a wedge-shaped Mount

Baker Recreation Area of 8,473 acres on the south slope of the mountain. The tip of the wedge reaches nearly 10,000 feet at the rim of Sherman Crater. The powerful snowmobile lobby demanded access to the mountain, and the recreation area was established to accommodate this. Howard Appollonio was co-leader of the drive for a Mount Baker Wilderness with Ken Wilcox, and Appollonio says today that despite the compromises conservationists achieved 75% of their goal. As a map of the area reveals, decades of roadbuilding created numerous "cherry stems" that precluded establishment of a block of wilderness. Much of the eastern edge of the wilderness connects to the North Cascades National Park and its Stephen Mather Wilderness (the wilderness designation bestowed upon the park by Congress in 1988). The western reach of the roadless North Cascades had at last achieved a significant measure of protection, and the scenic climax of Mount Baker itself was preserved.

Mount Baker ski lift.

13

Present and Future

*The world is circumscribed. The surface of this little earth of ours is limit-
ed, and we cannot add to it . . . . All we can do is to turn it to the best possible account. Now, let us remember that the quality of natural beauty in the
world, the number of spots calculated to give enjoyment in the highest form,
are limited, and are being constantly encroached upon.*

— James Bryce, 1913

Forces of change are constantly at work on Mount Baker and its surroundings. Each fall and winter intense storms roar in off the Pacific, pounding the region with high winds and heavy rain. Debris washes into creeks
becoming dams which back up water into ponds that ultimately burst and
send floods downhill and downstream filling old culverts, blowing out roads,
burying salmon redds, and otherwise changing both natural and human-
made features of the landscape. Sometimes nature causes the change with no
help from people, at other times human impacts are part of the change. The
story told here is of a behemoth of nature, a large volcanic mountain lording
over its surroundings, and humans playing and working around and on it.
Over the course of the story the human power to bring change has increased
as technology has advanced and human numbers have grown. Will this trend
continue? Will change wrought by nature be the dominant story? One can
only look at the past and speculate about the future.

Since the arrival of the English and Americans early in the story, change
has been slow but steady and has taken many forms. Logging, mining, road-
building, trail-building, and recreation have all been part of the story. Recent
years have seen less logging, mining and road-building and an expansion of
recreation. They have also been years of increasing glacial retreat, likely an
indirect consequence of human activity. Rapid growth of the human population on Earth and its pumping of gases into the atmosphere has contributed

to global warming of climate that is melting glaciers everywhere including Mount Baker. Fluctuations in weather, perhaps also related to climate change, have given the region record snows and, paradoxically, record warmth. The winter of 1998-1999 brought record snowfall to the Mount Baker Ski Area, which tallied 1,140 inches, or 95 feet.

Human activity has wrought other unexpected changes. After World War II the population of bald eagles that had long wintered on the Nooksack River dropped precipitously. Many stressors associated with human activity that destroyed habitat and reduced reproductive success led to this regal bird being ultimately listed as an endangered species. Eagles had gathered in late fall and early winter for eons on Northwest rivers to feed on spawning salmon but by the 1960s were becoming scarce. A campaign to restore eagles has brought them back.

The climate continues to change and an argument rages about what, if anything, to do about it. Some argue for action that will slow the rate of change while others argue such an effort is costly and futile and that humans should adapt as best they can to inevitably changing conditions. Glaciers are receding in the North Cascades at a historically unprecedented rate. Increasingly variable weather provides too much water at times, too little at others. Changes large and small, on global and local scales, with consequences for the nature of Koma Kulshan, continue apace as they always will.

Much of the story told here describes mountaineering on Mount Baker. This sport has continued to bring thousands of people to its slopes. The mountain is seen prominently on the horizon by millions of people, many of them Canadians who live on British Columbia's Lower Mainland. Their eyes are drawn to this mountain of often brilliantly white snow and ice on their horizon, beckoning them to visit, and they do. On nice summer weekends a continuous stream of climbers flows up the Coleman and Easton Glaciers. In winter snowmobiles zoom over glaciers in the Mount Baker National Recreation Area, sometimes traveling all the way to the summit. The mountaintop is in wilderness and off limits to snow machines, but patrolling a wilderness boundary up there at nearly 11,000 feet is impossible. Occasionally a machine falls into a crevasse, but the risk only makes the trip more exciting for winter snowmobilers as it does for summer climbers.

One human enterprise in the region, the Mount Baker Ski Area, has flourished. It reopened after World War II but suffered some rough years. By the early 1950s the Korean War was draining resources, and use of the area was reduced so much the state highway department once again considered closing the Mount Baker Highway above Shuksan during winter. Local businessmen came to the rescue: they bought out the struggling Mount Baker Lodge Company and formed a new one, the Mount Baker Recreation

Ptarmigan.

Company. Better capitalized and managed than its predecessor, the new company was able to install the chairlift equipment necessary to attract skiers and by 1957 the operation began to make money. Its major market proved to be Canadians from the Lower Mainland. Today, even with growth of major Canadian ski areas close to the Vancouver population center, Canadian skiers and snowboarders alike enjoy the slopes of the Mount Baker Ski Area.

Skiing grew rapidly in the late 1950s and the 1960s. Trying to keep up with demand and even increase it, the company installed many facilities. By mid-1965 a second chairlift was in operation; more were installed in 1968 and 1969, and the area could lift five thousand skiers each hour up the slopes. A sewage treatment plant and a day lodge were operating in 1971. The new sport of snowboarding appeared in the 1980s, and Mount Baker has proven to be one of the best snowboarding mountains in the region. It has become a mecca for the sport and its annual Legendary Banked Slalom race, begun in 1985, attracts competitors from all over the snowboarding world.

Little snow falls in some winters (1977 foremost among them) and in others so much snow, as in the record year 1998-1999, the area has to close so lift paths can be cleared in some stretches. In 2009 it featured eight chair-lifts and two ropetows. Once centered in Heather Meadows, the ski area has expanded to White Salmon below the Meadows where a day lodge opened in 1995 that serves as the base and core of the current operation. The ski business has progressed far since a few hardy enthusiasts hiked up to Heather Meadows in the late 1920s, when the Mount Baker Lodge lay quiet under massive snowdrifts, and they had all they could manage to get in a couple of runs each day. Today skiing is big business and will likely continue to be so.

The ski area today has no monopoly on skiing in the Mount Baker region. Advances in equipment and knowledge of avalanche hazard have opened the backcountry to skiers and snowboarders. Happy Fisher, Ben Thompson, and other pioneers of skiing Mount Baker would approve. Back in their day all skiing was backcountry skiing, and while they would surely have welcomed lifts, they would also be drawn to the beauty and challenge of the spacious slopes of Table Mountain and the many ridges reaching out to Mount Baker itself. On the mountain's south slopes they would be amazed to see snowmachines roaring up the slopes from Schreibers Meadows. Perhaps they would be amazed too with the ever steeper slopes and bigger drops being taken on by "extreme" snowboarders and skiers. Young adventurers are all over Table Mountain, Mount Herman, Ptarmigan Ridge and Shuksan Arm. Accidents have been few as knowledge of winter terrain has increased, but occasionally skiers have lost their lives in avalanches and other accidents. Winter recreation is an important part of the annual use of the Mount Baker region and that too will continue.

Logging, a very important activity in the region through much of its history, dropped off significantly in the 1990s. How did this happen? Prior to World War II the rate of timber harvest on public timberlands around Mount Baker was quite low. Policy was partly responsible for this, geography partly so. The history of the timber industry in the region from its beginning in the 19th century was governed by accessibility – trees most easy to harvest and transport to mills were cut first, then those less and less accessible meaning further inland and up into the mountains. That was the geography part. The policy was to harvest on public lands at a rate calculated to maintain the price of lumber. If too much was harvested on public land while there was a good inventory on private land, the market would be flooded and the price reduced. The plan was to harvest on private land and then move to public land while private inventories recovered, then go back to those, and so on in an infinitely renewable cycle. The cycle would maintain a supply based on demand and thus stabilize prices. Sustained yield management would also guarantee an unending flow of timber from the collective land base. This, at least, was the grand plan and theory.

This approach resulted in relatively minor harvest of timber on the national forest around Mount Baker prior to World War II. Harvest had gradually advanced up the Nooksack and Skagit valleys prior to the war but had barely penetrated the Baker area during the Great Depression and the war. After the war the situation changed rapidly. In 1950 the upper valley of the Middle Fork of the Nooksack River was almost as wild as it had been in the days of Edmund Coleman. The Deming Trail was a popular recreation route into the scenic region south of Mount Baker, but the valley had not been changed by the logger's saw. Pressure to log the valley increased in the postwar period until, in 1962, a great windstorm struck the Pacific Northwest and blew down many old trees. The forests of the Middle Fork did not escape, though damage there was not as severe as in many other areas. Still, the timber industry and those in the Forest Service who had long wished to log the valley argued that they must go in and salvage the blow-downs before they were wasted. A road and logging camp were established in the upper Middle Fork. The road reached up the valley in the mid-1960s, and logging was extensive in subsequent decades. Spur roads reached high on the ridges on both sides of the river and up tributary streams. Clearcuts were carved high on Marmot and Grouse ridges immediately west of the main uplift of Mount Baker.

Logging roads also moved into virgin timber and up toward timberline to the east in the Baker River Ranger District. In a major development, a private utility company built a hydroelectric dam on the upper Baker River, and in 1959 the five-thousand-acre basin behind the dam was filling, enlarging the old Baker Lake that Joe Morovits knew so well. As part of this development thrust, roads for logging and recreation were constructed, one reaching six miles up Swift Creek to Baker Hot Springs, another ten miles up to Shuksan Creek, and a third nine miles up Sulphur Creek to Schreibers Meadows not far from timberline on Baker's south slope. These roads increased use of this scenic area in summer, and with the advent of snow machines brought users into the area in winter as well. The idea of extending the Shuksan Creek Road to meet the Mount Baker Highway was seriously enough considered to make its way into the recommendations of the North Cascades Study Report in 1965, but the idea was too impractical and expensive to be implemented.

When the Washington State Wilderness Act of 1984 was approved by Congress, one of its goals was to "release" national forest land not designated as wilderness or other special management for timber harvest. This goal was obviously important to the timber industry, which had been trying for years to see the wilderness issue resolved so it could get its saws into the rest of the forest. Celebration that the Wilderness Act of 1984 would finally achieve the goal of release was short-lived because, soon after the legislation was approved, another issue appeared that stopped timber development. The issue was protection of biological diversity. The National Forest Management

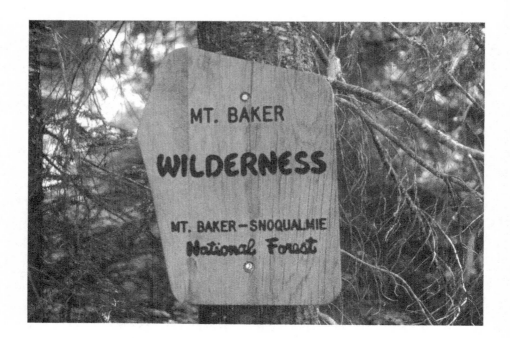

Act of 1976 (NFMA) directed the Forest Service to "provide for diversity of plant and animal communities." Six years later the Forest Service adopted regulations to meet this mandate. They included measures to maintain viable populations of vertebrate species and protect habitat for these species. Since assessing the viability of all species was an impossibly large job, "management indicator species" would be chosen, which would be used to indicate the condition of forest habitats and the organisms that depended on them. One species chosen to indicate the condition of late-stage succession or "old growth" forests in the Pacific Northwest was the northern spotted owl.

By the mid-1980s nearly all old growth forest outside of public land had been logged. Old growth forests tended to have the largest trees in them, so they were much coveted by timber companies. Any old growth forest to be preserved would be on public land, and even there the fate of what remained was uncertain. The Forest Service, trying to satisfy all of its stakeholders, thought more old growth could be logged. One provision of the NFMA was that the Forest Service should prepare comprehensive long range forest plans, which it was having difficulty doing in the face of the wilderness and now biodiversity issues. Keith Ervin nicely summed up the agency's fix:

> Planning was difficult in part because the Forest Service was shooting at a moving target. Before much work could be done on

the plans, RARE II . . . had to be completed. Until RARE II was translated into wilderness bills, national forest planners didn't know how large their commercial land base would be. In Oregon, Washington, and California, biologists were warning that the northern spotted owl required hundreds of thousands of acres of virgin timber to survive. The national forests couldn't complete their management plans until the Forest Service chief decided on a plan for the owl's protection. That plan – sure to generate a lawsuit by conservation groups – wasn't adopted until December 1988.[1]

Environmentalists seized on the spotted owl's decline and biologist's calculations of habitat needed to sustain it as a way to keep low-elevation national forests out of the commercial timber base and filed suit as predicted with the release of the forest plan. A federal judge enjoined the Forest Service from offering any large blocks of old growth as timber sales. This meant that in the Mount Baker region, as throughout the range of the owl, timber harvest on roadless blocks could not begin. There would be no release.

While the owl took the brunt of the fury from timber interests, the bird was only the "poster child" for a new view of the value of public lands in general. It was not the only organism threatened by possible elimination of an entire old growth forest-dependent community. Another bird, the marbled murrelet, was also at risk in the Mount Baker region, and concern was growing that activity in the uplands around salmon-bearing streams was threatening important stocks of this iconic fish. The NFMA had placed protection of biological diversity in the spectrum of considerations the Forest Service needed to include in its planning, and this was forcing a new approach to management focused on conservation of species and ecosystems. No longer could the Forest Service in the Mount Baker region consider primarily timber and recreation as the most important multiple uses in its planning. It now had to incorporate principles of landscape ecology and conservation biology. These perspectives were so new the Forest Service barely knew how to work with them, and failed in its planning for management of the northern spotted owl (at least in the court's eyes). Flow of timber off public land in the Mount Baker region virtually stopped.

The owl was listed as a threatened species under the Endangered Species Act in 1990 and in 1991 lawsuits over timber sales led to another injunction that shut down the timber sale program on nine national forests, the Mount Baker-Snoqualmie among them. The situation became so volatile that President Clinton convened a conference in Portland in April 1993 that directed federal land management and regulatory agencies to come up with a plan that would protect the ecological health of the forest while maintaining the benefits of a timber industry. Out of this came the Northwest Forest Plan in 1994 that has affected management of approximately 24 million acres of federal forest land. The Plan established late successional reserves which are managed to protect and enhance habitat for species, such as the northern spotted owl, that depend on mature forest. What this has meant for the Mount Baker region in the fifteen years since adoption of the Plan is very

Winter hiking at Artist Point.

little timber harvest on the Mount Baker Ranger District. The Forest Service is managing much of its forest outside wilderness to maintain or restore older forests. Not long ago, in the 1980s heyday of logging, trucks roared down the extensive system of forest roads in the region. Today these roads are little traveled. Many are not maintained. The Forest Service, its role as a timber supplier curtailed, cannot keep them up.

So what, in light of all of this, can be said of the future of Mount Baker and its surrounding landscape? Certainly various interest groups will continue to contend over how natural resources should be managed. They will argue over priorities, and the Forest Service will struggle to sort out the competing interests. It will probably try to keep all interests satisfied but will fail in this futile effort as it has in recent decades. Two conservation initiatives are under way in 2010, one to expand North Cascades National Park (at the expense of national forest jurisdiction) and one to expand national forest wilderness in the region. As long as there are people who wish to convert forests to commodities and others who wish to preserve them in their natural state, the arguments will continue and the Forest Service will be in the middle. Much reduced in the region by the virtual loss of its timber program, the agency will struggle with less budget and fewer professionals to "manage" what remains a large and important part of the northwest Washington landscape. Its planning for the future will continue to be fraught with many uncertainties. Back in 1981 it said, in its Draft Pacific Northwest Region Plan, that:

> The region does not have the capability to meet projected demand for wilderness-type use within the wilderness system. Wilderness use will increase not only as a function of population but also as use in presently undeveloped areas is displaced by other resource activities. By approximately the year 1985, the Region will not have the capability to meet the demand for this type of recreation within the wilderness system.[2]

Admittedly this statement refers to the entire Pacific Northwest, but in relation to the Mount Baker area it reveals the challenge of long-range planning there. Only three years after this draft the wilderness resource was enhanced by the Washington State Wilderness Act. The "other resource activities" it referred to in "presently undeveloped areas" are road-building and timber harvesting in roadless areas, a process that was stopped by the combination of wilderness legislation and concern for conservation of biological diversity.

The demand for timber from the National Forests was predicted in a 1980 Congressional Budget Office study to rise with consequences for remaining old growth and the long-term viability of the timber supply.

Several studies have concluded that (in the Pacific Northwest) the stock of second-growth timber will be too small to replace the decline of old-growth inventories and maintain production levels from private lands through the next 5 to 20 years. Consequently, allocation of a larger portion of the present inventory of National Forest old growth to sales during the 1980s would greatly increase the possibility of regional shortages in 10 to 30 years, if the increase in National Forest sales cannot be sustained.[3]

What this seems to say in lay terms is that the plan to maintain an even flow of timber to the marketplace, a policy goal for years for the Forest Service and timber industry, was threatened thirty years ago. The supply of old growth trees that had sustained the industry was depleted, and cutting more of it rapidly would mean shortages in the near future. The Forest service had tried to regulate timber harvest to assure what it called a "nondeclining even flow" to indefinitely maintain a stable timber supply, but had been pressured to cut more than could be sustained (especially when some of its timber base was taken away by wilderness designation). The pressure was on in 1980 to continue unsustainable harvest rates. As it turned out, harvest did increase for a time in the 1980s but so did concern that too much was being lost in the process. The result, with wilderness designation and measures to protect biological diversity, was that much old growth was preserved and the flow of logs slowed to a trickle in the Mount Baker region. The 1980 prediction proved prescient, but for reasons the forecasters did not predict. The policy of "nondeclining even flow" was frustrated. All of this illustrates the difficulty of trying to plan for the future in such a constantly changing and complex social, natural, and economic environment. The Forest Service struggles with this challenge today.

One huge potential for change in the future has nothing to do with the vagaries of human wants, needs and aspirations, and that is volcanism. Mount Baker is a volcano, and no one can predict when the mountain will become more active though most experts think that it will. It is, in geologic terms, a young volcano. As Mount St. Helens so dramatically demonstrated in 1980, such a volcano might violently spring to life at any time with little warning.

Mount Baker's activity could take many forms. Geologists have found evidence of several types of activity: toxic gas emissions, lava flows, earthquakes, mudflows, rock avalanches and pyroclastic flows (a mass of hot, dry rock debris moving viscously downslope under the influence of gravity). Any of these events, along with associated floods from melting glaciers, could occur in an eruptive episode. Increased thermal activity, constantly present at low levels, might be the first sign that something was brewing. Geologists

Climber silhouetted against building weather.

would respond (as they did in 1975 when just such an increase occurred) by installing monitoring equipment on the mountain to measure gas composition, heat, tilt of slopes and seismic activity. If significant temperature increase or earthquakes within the mountain were detected, people could be warned in areas that might be affected by an eruption, such as those living on the floodplains of the Nooksack and Skagit Rivers. People in Glacier or at Baker Lake might be evacuated. The mountain would be closed to climbing, hiking, skiing, and snowmobiling.

The most likely geologic outcomes of a volcanic "episode" on the mountain would be mudflows and rock avalanches. A rock debris avalanche, such as might come off Sherman Peak, could trigger a mudflow. A worst case might be such a mudflow going down Boulder Glacier into Baker Lake or down the Easton or Deming glaciers into the Middle Fork valley. Such slides, or lahars as geologists call them, might come off the western and northern sides of the mountain, moving as they have in the past down Glacier Creek to the present town of Glacier and beyond. Worst-case scenarios might have lahars burying Glacier or sliding into Baker Lake, displacing enough water to threaten Baker River dams, releasing impounded water and creating floods in the lowlands downstream.

In 1975 the increased thermal activity in Sherman Crater caused a lake of melted snow and glacier ice to be impounded. Geologists feared the resulting heat might weaken already unstable mud and rock in the crater and with the pressure of water and leakage into the unconsolidated volcanic material comprising the east side of the crater, result in a slide into Baker Lake. Precautions were taken around the lake, but the water drained harmlessly away. Life everywhere is fraught with uncertainty from weather, climate, and a multitude of human-generated unknowns. Life in the neighborhood of a geologic behemoth like Mount Baker offers unusual uncertainties along with the many positive values. Life with a volcano is not without its risks, long-term though they may be.

A futurist once predicted that the future will be like the past, or only more so, and this may be the case for Koma Kulshan. On the other hand, with emergence of concern for declining biological diversity, a weakened Forest Service, and global climate change melting the mountain's glaciers, the future may be very different from the recent past. Extractive natural resource industries have declined in the past few decades, and with the human population in the Pacific Northwest growing rapidly, the recreational value of the region will increase. With wilderness designation of much of the area, the prospect of industrial development has lessened, but other as yet unimagined landscape-changing development may appear.

One certainty is that the gleaming mountain on the horizon will continue to inspire with its beauty and challenge with its power and mystery. Climbers will continue to come, some only to "conquer" this one peak that intrudes on their consciousness, others to add it to their bag of peaks climbed. Pioneers in the sport of mountaineering have long since moved on to challenges on bigger mountains across the world, but they will still come to Baker for fun, to paraglide and ice climb and ski and snowboard ever-steeper slopes. The "groove" will be carved into Coleman Glacier above Glacier Creek by the average climber bent simply on the summit, at least when the road to trailhead is open, which has been a problem as Mother Nature has recently launched a campaign to take back the North Cascades by washing out access roads.

The history of Koma Kulshan has been one of conquest. Before the conquerors arrived – before history – Native Americans lived for thousands of years in the landscape, changing it in relatively minor ways, making the place their home. British and later American explorers, trappers, prospectors, miners, loggers, settlers, and developers of all kinds came to withdraw resources from nature's bank. Climbers, hikers, and tourists came to enjoy and be inspired by the grand scenery of verdant forests, cathedral stands of trees, abundant waterfalls, and the grandeur of big glaciated mountains. They came to be challenged and inspired. Some of these had visions of parks and wilderness, some of which were realized. The history of this place is rich, a natural and cultural history that is the legacy of Americans but especially of those who live within sight of Mount Baker. The future of Koma Kulshan will, without doubt, be as interesting as its past.

Endnotes

Chapter 1

1 Many details of Coleman's attempts on Mount Baker are from his article "Mountaineering on the Pacific," *Harpers New Monthly Magazine* 39 (November 1869): 793-817. The entire article with notations is in Harry Majors, ed., *Mount Baker: a Chronicle of its Historic Eruptions and First Ascent* (Seattle: Northwest Press, 1978).

2 Harry M. Majors, ed. *Mount Baker: A Chronicle of its Historic Eruptions and First Ascent* (Seattle: Northwest Press, 1978), p. 68.

3 Stratton, "Ascent of Mount Baker," *The Weekly Message* (Port Townsend), September 3, 1868, p. 2, and September 10, 1868, p. 1.

4 Ibid.

5 Ibid.

6 Ibid.

7 Majors, *Mount Baker*, pp. 202-7, describes what is known of Coleman's post-Mount Baker career.

Chapter 2

1 June McCormick Collins, *Valley of the Spirits: The Upper Skagit Indians of Western Washington* (Seattle: University of Washington Press, 1974), pp. 21-2. Recent work by North Cascades National Park archaeologist Bob Mierendorf and his colleagues suggests that Native Americans ventured into the high country in the early Holocene, following retreat of the last Cordilleran Ice Sheet, approximately 10,000 years ago. See Robert Mierendorf, *Archaeology of the Little Beaver Watershed, North Cascades National Park Service Complex, Whatcom County, Washington*. North Cascades National Park Service Complex, U.S. Department of Interior, Sedro Woolley, WA, 2004.

2 Allan H. Smith, *Ethnography of the North Cascades*. North Cascades National Park Service Complex and Cultural Resource Division, Pacific Northwest Region, Seattle, WA 1988.

3 Footnote by Charles M. Buchanan in Theodore Winthrop, *The Canoe and the Saddle* (Tacoma: Williams, 1913), p. 279. Quoted in Majors, *Mount Baker*, p. 16.

4 Brent Calloway and Allan Richardson, "Nooksack Place Names: An Ethnohistorical and Linguistic Approach," *Working Papers for the 18th International Conference on Salish and Neighboring Languages* (Seattle: University of Washington Press, August 1983).

5 Collins, *Valley of the Spirits*, p. 157.

6 Smith, *Ethnography of the North Cascades*, pp. 46-8.

7   Charles M. Buchanan, "The Origin of Mounts Baker and Rainier: The Indian Legend," *The Mountaineer, 9* (December 1916): 32-5.

8   Ella F. Clark, *Indian Legends of the Pacific Northwest* (Berkeley: University of California Press, 1953), p. 8. Recent research suggests that earlier theories that Indians would not venture high into the mountains were incorrect. Mierendorf has found archaeological evidence of Indian activity at upper elevations in the Cascades and thus such "legends" as those cited by Clark may be misleading. Sliuskin may have been entertaining his clients.

9   Ibid.

10 Ibid., p. 43.

11 Charles Finley Easton, "Mount Baker – Its Trails and Legends: Original Discovery of the Entrance to Puget Sound and First View of Mount Baker," *Northwest Journal of Education*, 25, 4.

12 Robert Ballard Whitebrook, *Coastal Explorations of Washington* (Palo Alto: Pacific Books, 1959, pp. 54-63.

13 Majors, *Mount Baker*, p. 12.

14 George Vancouver et. al., *A Voyage of Discovery to the North Pacific Ocean* (London, 1798), vol. 1, pp. 221-222.

15 Collins, *Valley of the Spirits*, p. 32

16 F.W. Howay, W.N. Sage and H.F. Angus, *British Columbia and the United States* (Toronto: The Ryerson Press, 1942) p. 142.

17 Ibid.

Chapter 3

1   Robert Emmett Hawley, *Skquee Mus: Pioneer Days on the Nooksack* (Bellingham: Whatcom Museum of History and Art, 1971), p. xxi.

2   Easton, "Mount Baker: Its Trails and Legends," Whatcom Museum of History and Art, Bellingham (Unpublished scrapbook, compiled 1903-1930), p. 42.

3   Ibid.

4   Ibid.

5   Tillicum (pseudonym for L.L Bales), "A Trip to Mount Baker," *Pacific Magazine* 2 (March 1890), pp. 8-9.

6   Ibid.

7   Majors, *Mount Baker*, pp. 208-9.

8   "Ascent of Mount Baker," *The West Shore* 10 (August 1884), 237.

9   Ibid.

10 Frank Carleton Teck, "Mountain Climbers Who Have Ascended Mount Baker," *Seattle Post-Intelligencer,* July 29, 1906.

11 Easton, p. 43.

12 For the full story of the North Cascades Highway, see JoAnn Roe, *The North Cascadians* (Seattle: Madrona Publishers, 1980).

13 Quoted in Percival R. Jeffcott, *Cheechaco and Sourdough* (Bellingham: Pioneer Printing Company, 1963), p. 20.

ENDNOTES

Chapter 4

1 *Whatcom Reveille,* July 8, 1891.
2 Aubrey Haines, *Mountain Fever* (Portland: Oregon Historical Society, 1962), p. 225 (footnote).
3 Easton, p. 48.
4 Ibid.
5 Ibid.
6 Ibid., p. 50.
7 A fine work on Hegg is Murray Morgan, *One Man's Gold Rush* (Seattle: University of Washington Press, 1967).
8 Easton, p. 54.
9 Ibid.
10 Ibid.
11 Ibid.
12 Dolly Connelly, "Morovits: The Hospitable Hermit of Baker Lake," *Off Belay,* 26 (August 1976), pp. 6-10.
13 A.J. Craven, "Morovits: The Hermit of Baker Lake," in Easton, p. 214.
14 Ibid.

Chapter 5

1 Easton, p. 57.
2 Accounts of the Heliograph expedition are from Frank Branch Riley, "Struggle with Mount Baker," *Mazama* (1948), p. 51, and M.W. Gorman's letter to Easton, in Easton, p. 59.
3 Ibid., p. 52.
4 Jeffcott, *Cheechaco and Sourdough,* p. 76.
5 Ibid., pp. 83-4.
6 Ibid., p. 83.
7 *Whatcom Reveille,* September 22, 1897.
8 Mary DeBorde, "Glacier: A History" (Glacier, Washington: Mount Baker-Snoqualmie National Forest, 1981), p. 73 (mimeographed).
9 Ibid.
10 Harold C. Criswell, "Historical Sketch – Mount Baker National Forest," *The Mountaineer,* 57, 4 (March 1964), pp. 48-9.
11 Ibid., p. 53.
12 The name of this institution, which appears in the Mount Baker story at several stages, was initially the State Normal School at New Whatcom, changed to the State Normal School at Whatcom in 1901, to Western College of Education in 1937, Western Washington State College in 1960-61, and Western Washington University in 1977.
13 C.E. Rusk, *Tales of a Western Mountaineer* (Boston: Houghton Mifflin Company, 1924), pp. 117-135.

Chapter 6

1   John D. Scott, *We Climb High* (Portland: The Mazamas, 1969), p. 13.
2   Ibid.
3   Ibid.
4   Asahel Curtis, "The First Ascent of Mount Shuksan," from *Overland Monthly* (August 1907), in Easton, p. 70.
5   Ibid.
6   Ibid.
7   R.L. Glisan, "A Night on the Summit of Mount Baker," in Easton, p. 88.
8   Ibid.
9   "With the Mountaineers on Mount Baker," *The Mountaineer*, 1, 4 (1908), p. 10.
10 Easton, "Storm Bound on Mt. Baker," *Forest and Stream*, LXXII, 1 (January 2, 1909), p. 10.
11 Gertrude Metcalfe Sholes, "The Mount Baker Outing of the Mazamas in 1909," *Mazama*, VI, 1 (December 1920), p. 28.
12 Ibid.
13 Ibid., p. 30.

Chapter 7

1   *American –Reveille* (Bellingham), July 11, 1912, editorial.
2   Ibid., August 11, 1911, p. 2.
3   Ibid., July 13, 1912, editorial.
4   Ibid, July 7, 1912, p. 7.
5   Ibid., July 25, 1912, p. 3.

Chapter 8

1   Scott, *We Climb High*, p. 13.
2   Easton, p. 193.
3   From "official correspondence," quoted by Easton, p. 194.
4   Ibid.
5   Easton, p. 196.
6   Ibid.
7   Ibid.
8   Ibid., p. 205.
9   See Harold K. Steen, *The U.S. Forest Service: A History*, Centennial Edition. (Seattle: Forest History Society in Association with the University of Washington Press, 2004), pp. 113-122.
10 For a more detailed description of the Mount Baker Lodge, see Ramon Heller, *Mount Baker Ski Area: A Pictorial History* (Bellingham: Mount Baker Recreation Company, 1980).
11 Fred H. McNeil, "Backtracking Old Trails," *Mazama*, XII 12 (December, 1930), p. 9.

12 L.R. Frazeur, "With the Mountaineers in 1916," *The Mountaineer*, 9 (December 1916), p. 13.
13 Jamieson Parker, "The Mount Baker Outing of 1920," *Mazama*, VI 1 (December 1920), pp. 3-15.
14 Easton, p. 214.
15 Connelly, "Morovits," p. 10.
16 *Bellingham Herald*, July 11, 1960.

Chapter 9
1 See Heller, *Mount Baker Ski Area*, pp. 29-46.
2 Deborde, "Glacier," pp. 78-82.
3 Deborde, "Glacier," pp. 71-72.
4 H.H. Long, "Mount Baker Forest Created in 1897, Embraces 1,851,397 Acres," *Bellingham Herald*, June 1940.

Chapter 10
1 Fred Beckey, *Challenge of the North Cascades* (Seattle: The Mountaineers, 1969), pp. 199-200.
2 Ed Cooper, "Climbing Notes," *The Mountaineer*, 1958, pp. 101-2.
3 Fred Beckey, "Climbs and Expeditions," *American Alpine Club Journal*, 1959, p. 305.
4 Ed Cooper, "Climbing Notes," *The Mountaineer*, 1961, p. 100.
5 Anton Karuza, "Climbing Notes," *The Mountaineer*, 1977, p. 106.
6 Klint Vielbig, "Climbing Notes," *The Mountaineer*, 1961, pp. 99-100.
7 Ed Cooper, "Climbs and Expeditions – Mount Baker," *American Alpine Club Journal*, 1959, p. 146.
8 Herb Staley, "Climbs and Expeditions – Mount Baker, Lincoln Peak," *American Alpine Club Journal* 1957, p. 146.
9 Ibid., p. 147.
10 Ibid.
11 Ibid., p. 148.
12 Herb Staley, "Climbing Notes," *The Mountaineer*, 1956, p. 121.
13 Ibid.

Chapter 11
1 William N. Parke, "Report on the 1939 Mount Baker Avalanche Rescue Work" (Washington: Government Printing Office, 1939), p. 4.

Chapter 12
1 Bert Huntoon, speech to Bellingham Chamber of Commerce, in *Mount Baker Scrapbook – 1930s*, Mount Baker Hiking Club, Bellingham, Washington.
2 Ibid.
3 B. H. Kiser, "Letter," in *Cascade Mountain Study* (Olympia: Washington State Planning Council, May, 1940).

4 Huntoon, op. cit.

5 J. Michael McCloskey, ed. *Prospectus for a North Cascades National Park* (Seattle: North Cascades Conservation Council, 1963.).

6 Orville Freeman and Stuart Udall, "Letter of January 28, 1963, from Secretary of the Interior and Secretary of Agriculture to President Kennedy," in North Cascades Study Team, *The North Cascades* (Washington, D.C.: U.S. Department of the Interior – U.S. Department of Agriculture, October, 1965), pp. 153-4.

7 Ibid., p. 16.

8 Ibid., pp. 134-5.

9 Ibid., p. 140.

10 Approved on October 2, 1968, Public Law 90-544 established North Cascades National Park, Ross Lake and Lake Chelan National Recreation Areas, designated the Pasayten Wilderness in the Okanogan National Forest, and enlarged the existing Glacier Peak Wilderness.

11 Doug Scott, *The Enduring Wilderness: Protecting Our Natural Heritage Through the Wilderness Act.* (Golden, CO: Fulcrum, 2004), p. 83.

Chapter 13

1 Keith Irvin, *Fragile Majesty: The Battle for North America's Last Great Forest* (Seattle: The Mountaineers, 1989), p. 185.

2 United States Department of Agriculture, Forest Service, "Draft Pacific Northwest Region Plan (Portland: Pacific Northwest Region, Forest Service, July 1981), p. 36.

3 Congressional Budget Office, "Forest Service Timber Sales: Their Effect on Wood Product Prices," May 1980.

Bibliography

Natural History

Alexander, G. "The Natural History of High Altitudes." *Biology* 33.3:91-97.

Bengtson, K.E. "Coleman Glacier Studies, Mount Baker." *Mountaineer* 13:36-7.

Burke, Raymond. "Neoglaciation of Boulder Valley, Mount Baker, Washington." Masters Thesis, Western Washington State College, 1972.

Dabenmire, R.F. "Ecologic Plan Geography of the Pacific Northwest." *Madroño* 20:3:111-28.

Davidson, George. "Recent Volcanic Activity in the United States." *Science* 6:262.

Dyson, James L. *The World of Ice*. New York: Alfred A. Knopf, 1962.

Easterbrook, Don J., and Rahm, David A. *Landforms of Washington*. Bellingham, Department of Geology, Western Washington State College, 1970.

Edwards, Ola. "Adaptations to Harshness: Alpine Plants in the Pacific Northwest." *Mountaineer* 48:57.

English, Edith Hardin. "Mammals of Austin Pass, Mt. Baker." *Mazama* 12:2:34-43.

Fries, Mary A. *Wildflowers of Mount Rainier and the Cascades*. Seattle: The Mountaineers and Mount Rainier Natural History Association, 1970.

Harris, Stephen L. *Fire and Ice: The Cascade Volcanoes*. Seattle: The Mountaineers and Pacific Search Press, 1976.

Harrison, A.E. "Fluctuations of the Coleman Glacier, Mt. Baker, Washington, USA." *Journal of Geophysical Research* 66:649-50.

____ "Climate and Glacier Fluctuations." *American Geophysical Union Transactions* 45:608.

____ "Short Notes on Fluctuations of Coleman Glacier, Mt. Baker, Washington, USA." *Journal of Glaciology* 9:393-6.

Hyde, Jack H., and Crandell, Dwight R. "Postglacial Volcanic Deposits of Mount Baker, Washington, and Potential Hazards from Future Eruptions." U.S. Geological Survey, Professional Paper 1022C, 1978.

Kozloff, Eugene N. *Plants and Animals of the Pacific Northwest*. Seattle: University of Washington Press, 1976.

Kritzman, Ellen B. *Little Mammals of the Pacific Northwest*. Seattle: Pacific Search Press, 1977.

Kruckeberg, Arthur R., *The Natural History of Puget Sound Country*. Seattle: University of Washington Press, 1991.

Long, W.A. "Mount Baker's Disappearing Glacier." *Summit* 4:6.

Lyons, C.P. *Trees, Shrubs and Flowers to Know in Washington*. Toronto: J.M. Dent and Sons, 1956.

McKee, Bates. *Cascadia: The Geologic Evolution of the Pacific Northwest*. New York: McGraw-Hill 1972.

Pojar, J., and MacKinnon, A. *Plants of the Pacific Northwest Coast: Washington, Oregon, British Columbia & Alaska*. Redmond, WA: Lone Pine Publishing, 1994.

Tabor, Rowland, and Haugerud, Ralph, *Geology of the North Cascades: A Mountain Mosaic*. Seattle: The Mountaineers, 1999.

Taylor, Ronald J., and Douglas, George W. *Mountain Wildflowers of the Pacific Northwest*. Portland: Binford and Mort, 1975.

Turekian, K.K., ed. *The Late Cenozoic Glacial Ages*. New Haven: Yale University Press, 1971.

Waitt, Richard B., Jr. "Evolution of Glaciated Topography of Upper Skagit Drainage Basin, Washington." *Arctic and Alpine Research* 9:2:185.

Wright, H. E., Jr, and Frey, D.G., eds. *The Quaternary of the United States*. Princeton: Princeton University Press, 1965.

Zwinger, Ann H., and Willard, Beatrice E. *Land Above the Trees*. New York: Harper and Row, 1972.

General History

Amoss, Pamela. "The Persistence of Aboriginal Beliefs and Practices Among the Nooksack Coast Salish." Ph.D. dissertation, University of Washington, 1972.

Avery, Mary W. *Washington: A History of the Evergreen State*. Seattle: University of Washington Press, 1965.

Beckey, Fred. *Range of Glaciers: The Exploration and Survey of the Northern Cascade Range*. Portland: Oregon Historical Society, 2003.

Clark, Ella F. *Indian Legends of the Pacific Northwest*. Berkeley: University of California Press, 1953.

Collins, June McCormick. *Valley of the Spirits: The Upper Skagit Indians of Western Washington*. Seattle: University of Washington Press, 1974.

Criswell, Harold C. "Historical Sketch: Mount Baker National Forest." *Mountaineer* 57:4:41-53.

DeBorde, Mary. "Glacier: A History." Glacier, Washington: Mt. Baker-Snoqualmie National Forest, 1981 (mimeographed).

Easton, Charles Finley. "Mt. Baker, Its Trails and Legends." Bellingham: Whatcom Museum of History and Art (unpublished scrapbook), compiled 1903-1940.

Ervin, Keith. *Fragile Majesty: The Battle for North America's Last Great Forest*. Seattle: The Mountaineers, 1989.

Field, Newton. *Mount Baker Almanac*. Bellingham: Mt. Baker-Snoqualmie National Forest, 1951 (mimeographed).

Hawley, Robert Emmett. *Squee Muss: Pioneer Days on the Nooksack*. Bellingham: Whatcom Museum of History and Art, 1971.

Heller, Ramon. *Mount Baker Ski Area: A Pictorial History*. Bellingham: Mount Baker Recreation Company, 1980.

Hirt, Paul W. *A Conspiracy of Optimism: Management of the National Forests Since World War Two*. Lincoln: University of Nebraska Press, 1992.

Howay, F.W.; Sage, W.N.; and Angus, H.F. *British Columbia and the United States*. Toronto: The Ryerson Press, 1942.

Jeffcott, Percival R. *Nooksack Tales and Trails*. Sedro-Woolley, Washington: Sedro-Woolley Courier Times, 1949.

___ *Cheechaco and Sourdough*. Bellingham: Pioneer Printing Company, 1963.

Johnson, Dorothy H., and Jeffcott, Percival R. *John A. Tennant: Early Pioneer and Preacher*. Bellingham: Fourth Corner Registry, 1978.

Judson, Katherine. *Myths and Legends of the Pacific Northwest*. Chicago: A.C. McClurg, 1910.

Majors, Harry M., ed. *Mount Baker: A Chronicle of Its Historic Eruptions and First Ascent*. Seattle: Northwest Press, 1978.

Meany, Edmond S. *History of the State of Washington*. New York: The Macmillan Company, 1910.

___ *Vancouver's Discovery of Puget Sound*. Portland: Binford and Mort, 1957.

Middleton, Lynn. *Place Names of the Pacific Northwest Coast*. Seattle: Superior Publishing Company, 1969.

Miles, John C., ed. *Impressions of the North Cascades: Essays about a Northwest Landscape*. Seattle: The Mountaineers, 1996.

Roe, JoAnn. *The North Cascadians*. Seattle: Madrona Publishers, 1980.

Roth, Dennis. *The Wilderness Movement and the National Forests*. College Station, Texas: Intaglio Press, 1988.

Roth, Lottie R. *History of Whatcom County*. Seattle: Pioneer Historical Publishing Company, 1926.

Schmierer, Alan C. *Northing Up the Nooksack*. Seattle: Pacific Northwest National Parks & Forests Association, 1983.

Scott, Doug. *The Enduring Wilderness: Protecting Our Natural Heritage Through the Wilderness Act*. Golden, CO: Fulcrum Publishing, 2004.

Smith, Marian W. "The Nooksack, the Chilliwack, and the Middle Fraser." *Pacific Northwest Quarterly* 41:330-41.

Steen, Harold K. *The U.S. Forest Service: A History*. Seattle: University of Washington Press, 1976.

Stern, Bernhard J. *The Lummi Indians of Northwest Washington*. New York: Columbia University Press, 1934.

Tremaine, David G. "Indian and Pioneer Settlement of the Nooksack Lowland, Washington." Masters thesis, Western Washington State College, 1975.

Whitebrook, Robert Ballard. *Coastal Explorations of Washington*. Palo Alto: Pacific Books, 1959.

Willis, Margaret, ed. *Cheechacos All: The Pioneering of the Skagit*. Mount Vernon, Washington: Skagit Historical Society, 1973.

Winthrop, Theodore. *The Canoe and the Saddle,* Nisqually Ed. Portland: Binfords & Mort, n.d.

Mountaineering History

Adams, W.C. "Reminiscences of Mt. Baker." *Mazama* 5:43:38-42.

Beckey, Fred. *Challenge of the North Cascades*. Seattle: The Mountaineers, 1969.

___ *Cascade Alpine Guide: Rainey Pass to Fraser River*. Seattle: The Mountaineers, 1981.

Cooper, Ed. "Climbing Notes: Mount Baker, Coleman Glacier Headwall." *Mountaineer* 51:4:101-2.

___ "Climbing Notes: Mount Baker, Roman Nose." *Mountaineer* 54:4:100.

Curtis, Asahel. "The Mountaineers' First Ascent of Mount Baker. *Mountaineer* 1:4:87-99.

Frazeur, Mrs. L.R. "With the Mountaineers in 1916." *Mountaineer* 9:7-24.

Jones, Chris. *Climbing in North America*. Berkeley: University of California Press, 1976.

Kjeldsen, Jim. *The Mountaineers: A History*. Seattle: The Mountaineers, 1998.

McNeil, Fred H. "Backtracking Old Trails" *Mazama* 12:2:7-20.

Meany, Edmond S. "The Ascent of Mount Baker, 1919." *Mountaineer* 12:42-4.

Miles, John C. "Mount Baker – 1868." *Off Belay* 38:2-5.

___ "Prospectors and Mountaineers." *Off Belay* 38:11-28.

Nettleton, Lulie. "With the Mountaineers on Mount Baker." *Mountaineer* 1:4: 88-96.

Parker, Jamieson. "The Mount Baker Outing of 1920." *Mazama* 6:1:3-15.

Rusk, C.E. *Tales of a Western Mountaineer*. Boston: Houghton Mifflin Company, 1924.

Scott, John D. *We Climb High*. Portland: The Mazamas, 1969.

Sholes, Gertrude Metcalfe. "The Mount Baker Outing of the Mazamas in 1909." *Mazama* 6:1:26-32.

Other Sources

Connelly, Dolly. "New Playground for 1960: Mount Baker's South Side." *Seattle Times*, November 29, 1959.

___ "Morovits" The Hospitable Hermit of Baker Lake." *Off Belay* 28:6-10.

___ "The Mount Baker Marathon." *Off Belay* 7:2-7.

Frome, Michael. *Whose Woods These Are*. Garden City, New Jersey: Doubleday & Company, Inc., 1962.

Hazard, Joseph T. *Snow Sentinels of the Pacific Northwest*. Seattle: Lowman & Hanford Co., 1932.

Moen, Wayne S. *Mines and Mineral Deposits of Whatcom County, Washington*. Olympia: State of Washington, Department of Natural Resources, 1969.

Mount Baker Club Scrapbooks, 1930-1970.

Parke, William N. "Report on the 1939 Mount Baker Avalanche Rescue Work." Washington: Government Printing Office, 1940.

Smith, Allan H. *Ethnography of the North Cascades*. Pullman: Center for Northwest Anthropology, Washington State University, 1988.

Sucher, David, ed. *The Asahel Curtis Sampler.* Seattle: Puget Sound Access, 1973.

Tobias, Michael Charles, and Drasdo, Harold, eds. *The Mountain Spirit.* Woodstock, New York: The Overlook Press, 1979.

U.S. Forest Service. "Analysis of National Forest Lands Included in a Proposal for a North Cascades National Park." Portland: Pacific Northwest Region, December 1962.

U.S. Forest Service. *Highlights in the History of Forest Conservation.* Washington: Government Printing Office, 1976.

U.S. Forest Service. "Report on the Recreation Resources of the National Forests in the North Cascades." Portland: Pacific Northwest Region, 1963.

U.S. Forest Service. "Summary, Final Environmental Statement, Roadless Area Review and Evaluation." Washington, D.C.: Government Printing Office, 1979.

U.S. Department of the Interior and Department of Agriculture, North Cascades Study Team. *The North Cascades.* Washington, D.C.: Government Printing Office, 1965.

U.S. National Park Service and Western Washington University. *The North Cascades: An Environmental Symposium.* Bellingham: Western Washington University, 1976.

Index

INDEX

Photo Credits

Center for Pacific Northwest Studies, Western Washington University, Bellingham – pages 139, 145, 150, 151, 163, 172, 173; Sam Gardner – pages 197, 198; U.S. Forest Service Collection – pages 83, 167, 168-169, 170, 171; John Miles – cover insert, pages 7, 10, 14, 164, 178, 183, 184, 205, 209, 211, 217, 220, 222, 225; John Rupley – page 176; Western Washington University Archives, Bellingham – pages 189, 190; Whatcom Museum Archives, Bellingham – cover, pages 2, 12, 16, 19, 21, 22, 23, 27, 31, 40-41, 44, 49, 50, 52, 53, 54, 56, 57, 59, 60, 64, 67, 69, 72, 74, 85, 86, 88, 91, 95, 97, 100, 103, 105, 107, 108, 109, 110, 112, 116-117, 120, 125, 127, 128, 132, 134, 141, 143, 149, 152-153, 154, 157, 158, 160, 162, 165, 180, 186, 214; Galen Biery, Whatcom Museum Archives, Bellingham – pages 20, 78, 122-123, 124, 126, 187.

About the Author

John C. Miles, a resident of Bellingham, Washington, gazes at Mount Baker on every clear day. He first climbed the mountain in 1968 and has made many ascents since. An avid climber, hiker, and skier, he has cultivated first hand knowledge of the peak, constantly doing "research" in pursuit of academic fame and fortune.

Miles is Professor of Environmental Studies at Western Washington University's Huxley College of the Environment. He has served as chair of the Department of Environmental Studies as well as Dean of the College. His books include *Guardians of the Parks: A History of the National Parks and Conservation Association* (1995), *Impressions of the North Cascades* (1996), and *Wilderness in National Parks: Playground or Preserve* (2009).

CPSIA information can be obtained
at www.ICGtesting.com
Printed in the USA
BVOW09s1452110418
513077BV00006B/533/P

9 780984 238934